SLOW TIME

100 Poems to Take You There

The Arts Council
An Chomhairle Ealaíon

Published in 2000 by Marino Books
An imprint of Mercier Press
16 Hume Street Dublin 2
Tel: (01) 661 5299; Fax: (01) 661 8583
E-mail: books@marino.ie

Trade enquiries to CMD Distribution
55A Spruce Avenue
Stillorgan Industrial Park
Blackrock County Dublin
Tel: (01) 294 2556; Fax: (01) 294 2564
E-mail: cmd@columba.ie

ISBN 1 86023 130 6

10 9 8 7 6 5 4 3 2 1

A CIP record for this title is available from
the British Library

Cover design by Penhouse
Typset by *Deirdre's Desktop*
Printed in Ireland by ColourBooks,
Baldoyle Industrial Estate, Dublin 13

Slow Time

100 Poems to Take You There

EDITED BY

NIALL MacMonagle

For Mary and Catherine
and for Marybeth Joyce

Acknowledgements

I would like to thank Mary Clayton, Gavin Maloney, Cormac Kinsella, Rolly Dingle, Lindi Dingle, Marybeth Joyce, Marguerite McDonagh, Kate Bateman, Sharon O'Brien, Sue Flanagan, Malachi Friel, Barrie Cooke, Jane Casey and Jo O'Donoghue.

CONTENTS

'Reading ourselves away from ourselves'

The clock is a precise and accurate instrument. In the morning it alarms us; it measures and charts the seconds, minutes and hours throughout our day and reminds us that it is time to go to bed. Clock time is linear but Margaret Atwood tells us that 'time is not a line but a dimension.' This other time, multi-layered, allows us a place and space outside the linear flow. Then everyday, familiar time, marked by the ticking of the clock, gives way to another order of experience: special, rare, enriching moments that we cherish all the more for being different.

Surveys which measure life's stress and frazzle frequently offer remedies: yoga, massage, a walk by the sea, gardening . . . and the reading of poetry. Reading poetry – reading a poem a day – is the most manageable of all. And it's easy to see why poetry should have this effect. A poem, made and shaped in silence, more often than not offers a direct, personal voice and our reading a poem in 'silence and slow time' is a one-to-one experience. A connection is made where another mind, imagination, emotion, another's experience become ours.

In 'Gift' an old man working in his garden early on a summer's morning realises, with gratitude, that envy and evil have slipped away. In 'What's Left' a woman who has been ill for fifteen years with ME knows 'how to live through my life now' and, in a companion poem by the same poet, Kerry Hardie, realises that:

> even sickness is generous
> and takes you by the hand and sits you
> beside things you would otherwise have passed over.

Eiléan Ní Chuilleanáin stands beside her mother in Parma Cathedral and both look up at Coreggio's painting, *Assumption of the Virgin Mary*, high overhead in the Cupola. In 'Fireman's Lift', a memory poem, Ní Chuilleanáin shows us 'what love sees.' In 'The Wishing Tree', Seamus Heaney commemorates his mother-in-law, who, in the poet's transforming imagination, is assumed heavenwards. Rita Ann Higgins's poem 'He Leaves the Ironing Board Open' tells of how she visited her brother in England, a brother whom she hadn't seen for some years, and discovered that he lived in a mobile home near the motorway. Her poem brings us to the heart of loneliness: not only her brother's, but everyone's.

In August Kleinzahler's poem, 'Winter Ball', a man at one end of a basketball court plays his solitary game; six women play at the other end on a Californian, New Year's Day, afternoon. He plays seriously, while the others just clown around, their different ways of playing becoming more than a game, 'with dark coming on and the cold'. An old woman travelling through the dark on a train in Italy looks at the old man opposite and imagines his boyhood. Denise Levertov in 'Evening Train' says:

This man perhaps
is ten, putting in a few hours most days
in a crowded schoolroom, and a lot more
at work in the fields; a boy who's always
making plans to go fishing his first free day.

Loneliness, old age, the dwindling light are quietly captured here in a number of poems but there are also poems of deep delight, poems which glow with small but significant happinesses, as in Fleur Adcock's hymn to her son in 'On A Son Returned to New Zealand', Joan McBreen's finding something special in ordinary, small-town Ireland, Conor O'Callaghan's clear-sighted description of a closing-down town that doesn't blind him from 'making a fist of love and glimpsing new dawns', Eamon Grennan's surprise when:

Four deer lift up their lovely heads to me
in the dusk of the golf course I plod across
towards home

or Elizabeth Bishop telling us how marvellous it is to wake up together.

W.H. Auden writes about a perfect summer evening spent with friends in the country:

Where the sexy airs of summer,
The bathing hours and the bare arms,
The leisured drives through a land of farms
Are good to a newcomer.

Thomas Kinsella focuses on love's continuity between mother and child; John Montague captures 'the sounds of Ireland, that restless whispering you never get away from', and Amy Clampitt, visiting a monastery in Greece, sees 'the plane trees . . . huge as churches, they might go back a thousand years . . . the light all muzzy silver . . .'

These, and the other poems in this collection, create a space of their own. When you read them you will read them in a particular place and at a particular time – on the bus, stuck in traffic, during a break in the office, on a park bench, at home – but the poems will allow you to forget yourself, the hurry you're in, the clock that keeps ticking and, like Auden's gloriously evocative poem which recreates a special summer's night, the poems in *Slow Time* may make possible a time, however brief, when:

> Fear gave his watch no look;
> The lion griefs loped from the shade
> And on our knees their muzzles laid,
> And Death put down his book.

Niall MacMonagle

Gift

A day so happy.
Fog lifted early, I worked in the garden.
Hummingbirds were stopping over honeysuckle flowers.
There was no thing on earth I wanted to possess.
I knew no one worth my envying him.
Whatever evil I had suffered, I forgot.
To think that once I was the same man did not embarrass
    me.
In my body I felt no pain.
When straightening up, I saw the blue sea and sails.

Berkeley, 1971

CZESLAW MILOSZ

What's Left

for Peter Hennessy

I used to wait for the flowers,
my pleasure reposed on them.
Now I like plants before they get to the blossom.
Leafy ones — foxgloves, comfrey, delphiniums —
fleshy tiers of strong leaves pushing up
into air grown daily lighter and more sheened
with bright dust like the eyeshadow
that tall young woman in the bookshop wears,
its shimmer and crumble on her white lids.

The washing sways on the line, the sparrows pull
at the heaps of drying weeds that I've left around.
Perhaps this is middle age. Untidy, unfinished,
knowing there'll never be time now to finish,
liking the plants — their strong lives —
not caring about flowers, sitting in weeds
to write things down, look at things,
watching the sway of shirts on the line,
the cloth filtering light.

I know more or less
how to live through my life now.
But I want to know how to live what's left
with my eyes open and my hands open;
I want to stand at the door in the rain
listening, sniffing, gaping.
Fearful and joyous,
like an idiot before God.

KERRY HARDIE

The Horses

Let their hooves print the next bit of the story:
Release them, roughnecked
From the dark stable where
They rolled their dark eyes, shifted and stamped —

Let them out, and follow the sound, a regular clattering
On the cobbles of the yard, a pouring round the corner
Into the big field, a booming canter.

Now see where they rampage,
And whether they are suddenly halted
At the check of the line westward
Where the train passes at dawn —

If they stare at land that looks white in patches
As if it were frayed to bone (the growing light
Will detail as a thickening of small white flowers),
Can this be the end of their flight?
The wind combs their long tails, their stalls are empty.

EILÉAN NÍ CHUILLEANÁIN

Ghosts

We live the lives our parents never knew
when they sang 'Come Back to Sorrento':
driving west in the evening from Pompeii,
its little houses sealed up in a tomb
of ash and pumice centuries ago
and now exposed to the clear light of day,
we found an old hotel with a sea view
and Naples' lights reflected in the bay
where, with a squeal of seagulls far below,
white curtains blew like ghosts into the room.

DEREK MAHON

Nostalgia

Remember the 1340s? We were doing a dance called the
    Catapult.
You always wore brown, the colour craze of the decade,
and I was draped in one of those capes that were
    popular,
the ones with unicorns and pomegranates in
    needlework.
Everyone would pause for beer and onions in the
    afternoon,
and at night we would play a game called 'Find the
    Cow'.
Everything was hand-lettered then, not like today.

Where has the summer of 1572 gone? Brocade and
    sonnet
marathons were the rage. We used to dress up in the
    flags
of rival baronies and conquer one another in cold rooms
    of stone.
Out on the dance floor we were all doing the Struggle
while your sister practised the Daphne all alone in her
    room.
We borrowed the jargon of farriers for our slang.
These days language seems transparent, a badly broken
    code.

The 1790s will never come again. Childhood was big.
People would take walks to the very tops of hills
and write down what they saw in their journals without
    speaking.
Our collars were high and our hats were extremely soft.
We would surprise each other with alphabets made of
    twigs.
It was a wonderful time to be alive, or even dead.

I am very fond of the period between 1815 and 1821.
Europe trembled while we sat still for our portraits.
And I would love to return to 1901 if only for a
    moment,
time enough to wind up a music box and do a few dance
    steps,
or shoot me back to 1922 or 1941, or at least let me
recapture the serenity of last month when we picked
berries and glided through afternoons in a canoe.

Even this morning would be an improvement over the
    present.
I was in the garden then, surrounded by the hum of bees
and the Latin names of flowers, watching the early light
flash off the slanted windows of the greenhouse
and silver the limbs on the rows of dark hemlocks.

As usual, I was thinking about the moments of the past,
letting my memory rush over them like water
rushing over the stones on the bottom of a stream.
I was even thinking a little about the future, that place
where people are doing a dance we cannot imagine,
a dance whose name we can only guess.

BILLY COLLINS

Nocturne

After a friend has gone I like the feel of it:
The house at night. Everyone asleep.
The way it draws in like atmosphere or evening.

One o'clock. A floral teapot and a raisin scone.
A tray waits to be taken down.
The landing light is off. The clock strikes. The cat

comes into his own, mysterious on the stairs,
a black ambivalence around the legs of button-back
chairs, an insinuation to be set beside

the red spoon and the salt-glazed cup,
the saucer with the thick spill of tea
which scalds off easily under the tap. Time

is a tick, a purr, a drop. The spider
on the dining room window has fallen asleep
among complexities as I will once

the doors are bolted and the keys tested
and the switch turned up of the kitchen light
which made outside in the back garden

an electric room — a domestication
of closed daisies, an architecture
instant and improbable.

Eavan Boland

The Voice You Hear When You Read Silently

is not silent, it is a speaking-
out-loud voice in your head: it is *spoken*,
a voice is *saying* it
as you read. It's the writer's words,
of course, in a literary sense
his or her 'voice' but the sound
of that voice is the sound of *your* voice.
Not the sound your friends know
or the sound of a tape played back
but your voice
caught in the dark cathedral
of your skull, your voice heard
by an internal ear informed by internal abstracts
and what you know by feeling,
having felt. It is your voice
saying, for example, the word 'barn'
that the writer wrote
but the 'barn' you say
is a barn you know or knew. The voice
in your head, speaking as you read,
never says anything neutrally — some people
hated the barn they knew,
some people love the barn they know
so you hear the word loaded
and a sensory constellation
is lit: horse-gnawed stalls,
hayloft, black heat tape wrapping

a water pipe, a slippery
spilled *chirrr* of oats from a split sack,
the bony, filthy haunches of cows . . .
And 'barn' is only a noun — no verb
or subject has entered into the sentence yet!
The voice you hear when you read to yourself
is the clearest voice: you speak it
speaking to you.

THOMAS LUX

Crow's Nest

On Saint Stephen's day,
Near the cliffs on Horn Head,
I came upon a house,
the roof beams long since rotted into grass
and outside, a little higher than the lintels,
a crow's nest in a dwarf tree.

A step up from the bog
into the crown of the ark,
the nest is a great tangled heart;
heather sinew, long blades of grass, wool and a feather,
wound and wrought
with all the energy and art
that's in a crow.

Did crows ever build so low before?
Were they deranged, the pair who nested here,
or the other pair who built the house behind the tree,
or is there no place too poor or wild
to support,
if not life,
then love, which is the hope of it,
for who knows whether the young birds lived?

MOYA CANNON

House Style

When my grandmother looked into my mother's eyes
she saw what I see in my daughter's.

VONA GROARKE

Four Deer

Four deer lift up their lovely heads to me
in the dusk of the golf course I plod across
towards home. They're browsing the wet grass
the snow has left and, statued, stare at me
in deep silence and I see whatever light there is
gather to glossy pools in their eight mild,
barely curious but wary eyes. When one at a time
they bend again to feed, I can hear the crisp
moist crunch of the surviving grass
between their teeth, imagine the slow lick of a tongue
over whickering lips. They've come from the unlit
winter corners of their fright to find
a fresh season, this early gift, and stand
almost easy at the edge of the white snow islands and
lap the grey-green sweet depleted grass. About them
hangs an air of such domestic sense, the comfortable
hush of folk at home with one another, a familiar
something I sense in spite of the great gulf of strangeness
we must look over at each other. Tails flicker
white in thickening dusk and I feel their relief at
the touch of cold snow underfoot while their faces
nuzzle grass, as if, like birds, they had crossed
unspeakable vacant wastes with nothing but hunger
shaping their brains and driving them from leaf to
dry leaf, sour strips of bark, under a thunder of guns
and into the cold comfort of early dark. I've seen
their straight despairing lines cloven in snowfields

under storm, an Indian file of famished natives, poor
unprayed-for wanderers through blinding chill, seasoned
castaways in search of home ports, which they've found
at last, here on winter's verge between our houses and
their trees. All of a sudden, I've come too close. Moving
as one mind they spring in silent waves
over the grass, then crack snow with sharp hard
snaps, lightfooting it into the sanctuary of a pine grove
where they stand looking back at me, a deer-shaped
family of shadows against the darker arch of trees and
this rusting dusk. When silence settles over us again
and they bow down to browse, the sound of grass being
lipped, bitten, meets me across the space between us.
    Close
enough for comfort, they see we keep, instinctively, our
distance, sharing this air where a few last shards of
daylight still glitter in little meltpools or spread a skin
of brightness on the ice, the ice stiffening towards
    midnight
under the clean magnesium burn of a first star.

Eamon Grennan

34

New Gravity

Treading through the half-light of ivy
and headstone, I see you in the distance
as I'm telling our daughter
about this place, this whole business:
a sister about to be born,
how life's new gravity suspends in water.
Under the oak, the fallen leaves
are pieces of the tree's jigsaw;
by your father's grave you are pressing acorns
into the shadows to seed.

ROBIN ROBERTSON

History of World Languages

They spoke the loveliest of languages.
Their tongues entwined in Persian, ran
And fused. Words kissed, a phrase embraced,
Verbs conjugated sweetly. Verse began.
So Eve and Adam lapped each other up
The livelong day, the lyric night.

Of all known tongues most suasive
Was the Snake's. His oratory was Arabic,
Whose simile and rhetoric seduced her
('Sovran of creatures, universal dame').
So potent its appeal —
The apple asked for eating,
To eat it she was game.

Now Gabriel turned up, the scholars say,
Shouting in Turkish. Harsh and menacing,
But late. And sounds like swords were swung.
Fault was underlined, and crime defined.
The gate slammed with the clangour of his tongue.

Eden was gone. A lot of other things
Were won. Or done. Or suffered.
Thorns and thistles, dust and dearth.
The words were all before them, which to choose.
Their tongues now turned to English,
With its colonies of twangs.
And they were down to earth.

D. J. ENRIGHT

Cup

I no longer need to remember you
as I take out the two white cups
you gave me. Wide cups, from France.

Now I just look at a moon whiteness,
their silence. Waiting for the full
of rich roast coffee, the sugar, the cream.

I fill this emptiness. Savour the aroma
as I lift the cup to my lips.
And no longer taste, any vinegar.

ANNE LE MARQUAND HARTIGAN

Looking at Them Asleep

When I come home late at night and go in to kiss the
    children,
I see my girl with her arm curled around her head,
her face deep in unconsciousness — so
deeply centred she is in her dark self,
her mouth slightly puffed like one sated but
slightly pouted like one who hasn't had enough,
her eyes so closed you would think they have rolled the
iris around to face the back of her head,
the eyeball marble-naked under that
thick satisfied desiring lid,
she lies on her back in abandon and sealed completion,
and the son in his room, oh the son he is sideways in his
    bed,
one knee up as if he is climbing
sharp stairs up into the night,
and under his thin quivering eyelids you
know his eyes are wide open and
staring and glazed, the blue in them so
anxious and crystally in all this darkness, and his
mouth is open, he is breathing hard from the climb
and panting a bit, his brow is crumpled
and pale, his long fingers curved,
his hand open, and in the centre of each hand
the dry dirty boyish palm
resting like a cookie. I look at him in his
quest, the thin muscles of his arms

passionate and tense, I look at her with her
face like the face of a snake who has swallowed a deer,
content, content — and I know if I wake her she'll
smile and turn her face toward me though
half asleep and open her eyes and I
know if I wake him he'll jerk and say Don't and sit
up and stare about him in blue
unrecognition, oh my Lord how I
know these two. When love comes to me and says
What do you know, I say This girl, this boy.

SHARON OLDS

Windharp
for Patrick Collins

The sounds of Ireland,
that restless whispering
you never get away
from, seeping out of
low bushes and grass,
heatherbells and fern,
wrinkling bog pools,
scraping tree branches,
light hunting cloud,
sound hounding sight,
a hand ceaselessly
combing and stroking
the landscape, till
the valley gleams
like the pile upon
a mountain pony's coat.

JOHN MONTAGUE

Prognoses

'She'll walk something like this . . .'
Springing from his chair
he waddles, knees crumpled,
on the outer edges of his feet
 — a hunchback, jester, ape,
a wind-up toy
assembled by a saboteur.
I turn away, concentrate
on the caesarean sting.

I wander corridors.

Far off, approaching,
a couple, hand in hand,
the girl, lurching
against the window's light.
I hear them laugh, pick up
the drift — a private joke,
the film they saw last night.
Long after they are gone, I hear
the jaunty click-creak of her calipers.

CAROL SATYAMURTI

A Call

'Hold on,' she said, 'I'll just run out and get him.
The weather here's so good, he took the chance
To do a bit of weeding.'
              So I saw him
Down on his hands and knees beside the leek rig,
Touching, inspecting, separating one
Stalk from the other, gently pulling up
Everything not tapered, frail and leafless,
Pleased to feel each little weed-root break,
But rueful also . . .

              Then found myself listening to
The amplified grave ticking of hall clocks
Where the phone lay unattended in a calm
Of mirror glass and sunstruck pendulums . . .

And found myself then thinking: if it were nowadays,
This is how Death would summon Everyman.

Next thing he spoke and I nearly said I loved him.

SEAMUS HEANEY

The Magi

Toward world's end, through the bare
beginnings of winter, they are travelling again.
How many winters have we seen it happen,
watched the same sign come forward as they pass
cities sprung around this route their gold
engraved on the desert, and yet
held our peace, these
being the Wise, come to see at the accustomed hour
nothing changed: roofs, the barn
blazing in darkness, all they wish to see.

LOUISE GLÜCK

Bed-Time

Time to go to bed again. Time for the moon
To get in among the muddle of arms and legs,
    Get completely unstrung and set free
    And hold on to you. Because you've done
All this but are also the one thing
That'll hold me, lost in this narrow room

As if it's Pharaoh's mine of slippery agate,
    Flashing quartz chambers
Where I could wander for years

Now changed to an arch of green cedars
And a wild-honey garden of mist and secret walks
    With cyclamen in the shade, a tiltyard
    Of tiered lawns rising and rising — to sundials, mazes
And driftwood igloos seeing off dew from their walls
At dawn. Because of you. Because of you.

RUTH PADEL

Ways to Live
19 – 21 July

1 INDIA

In India in their lives they happen
again and again, being people or
animals. And if you live well
your next time could be even better.

That's why they often look into your eyes
and you know some far-off story
with them and you in it, and some
animal waiting over at the side.

Who would want to happen just once?
It's too abrupt that way, and
when you're wrong, it's too late
to go back — you've done it forever.

And you can't have that soft look when you
pass, the way they do it in India.

2 Having It Be Tomorrow

Day, holding its lantern before it,
moves over the whole earth slowly
to brighten that edge and push it westward.
Shepherds on upland pastures begin fires
for breakfast, beads of light that extend
miles of horizon. Then it's noon and
coasting toward a new tomorrow.

If you're in on that secret, a new land
will come every time the sun goes
climbing over it, and the welcome of children
will remain every day new in your heart.
Those around you don't have it new,
and they shake their heads turning grey every
morning when the sun comes up. And you laugh.

3 Being Nice and Old

After their jobs are done old people
cackle together. They look back and shiver,
all of that was so dizzying when it happened;
and now if there is any light at all it
knows how to rest on the faces of friends.
And any people you don't like, you just turn
the page a little more and wait while they
find out what time is and begin to bend
lower; or you can turn away
and let them drop off the edge of the world.

At night outside it all moves or
almost moves — trees, grass,
touches of wind. The room you have
in the world is ready to change.
Clouds parade by, and stars in their
configurations. Birds from far
touch the fabric around them — you can
feel their wings move. Somewhere under
the earth it waits, that emanation
of all things. It breathes. It pulls you
slowly out through doors or windows
and you spread in the thin halo of night mist.

WILLIAM STAFFORD

Timetable

We all remember school, of course:
the lino warming, shoe bag smell, expanse
of polished floor. It's where we learned
to wait: hot-cheeked in class, dreaming,
bored, for sour milk, for noisy now.
We learned to count, to rule off days,
and pattern time in coloured squares:
purple English, dark green Maths.

We hear the bells, sometimes,
for years, and heed the squeal
of white on black. We walk, don't run
in awkward pairs, hoping for the open door,
a foreign teacher, fire drill. And love's
long aertex summers, tennis sweat,
and somewhere, someone singing flat.
The art room, empty, full of light.

KATE CLANCHY

Hay

This much I know. Just as I'm about to make that right
    turn
off Province Line Road
I meet another beat-up Volvo
carrying a load

of hay. (More accurately, a bale of lucerne
on the roof rack,
a bale of lucerne or fescue or alfalfa.)
My hands are raw. I'm itching to cut the twine, to
    unpack

that hay-accordion, that hay-concertina.
It must be ten o'clock. There's still enough light
(not least from the glow

of the bales themselves) for a body to ascertain
that when one bursts, as now, something takes flight
from those hot and heavy box-pleats. This much, at
    least, I know.

Paul Muldoon

The Reservoirs of Mount Helicon

The monks are dying out at Hosios Loukas.
At Great Vespers the celebrant,
singing alone in a cracked ancient voice
while I hug the stall, sole auditor,
keeps losing his place in the chant-book's
stiff curled parchment. Having come by taxi
all the way from Delphi (the driver waits
outside, in no hurry) to be mowed down by a tsunami
of Greek voices, I experience only
the onset of an urge to giggle.
                      The mosaics
are hardly up to the postcards; tourists,
now that there's a highway, arrive
by the busload. But the ride up —
wet appletrees' cusp-studded wands
aped by the unlikely topside hue of crows
braking and turning just below eye-level —
is worth it, and so are the plane trees
that grow here: huge as churches,
they might go back a thousand years, be older
than Hosios Loukas, whose hermitage this was,
be older even than Luke the painter
of seraphic epiphanies. He'd have found it
strange here: the light all muzzy silver,
Helicon green and vast across a mist-
hung gorge, these plane trees
so palpably, venerably pagan —

but I think he might have liked it.
                                          Waiting
outside for the vesper bell, I fell into
conversation with a monk — one of fifteen
now remaining, he told me — who spoke a kind
of English learned, and since largely forgotten,
during a sojourn in Brooklyn. They'd been building
a bridge then, he recalled, across the Hudson;
he supposed it must be finished by now.
I told him, in a faint voice, yes,
it had been finished — and looked out, whelmed
into vertigo by gulfs spanned for a moment
by so mere a thread, across a gorge
already half-imaginary with distance
toward the improbable, the muse-haunted
reservoirs of Mount Helicon.

AMY CLAMPITT

Bella

'Her silences are my silences, her eyes, my eyes. It is as if Bella
had known me forever, as if she knew all my childhood, all my
present, all my future.'

Ma Vie, Marc Chagall

Now that I'm too old to hold a brush,
I paint you again each morning with words:
Double Portrait With Wine Glass,
Bella With Carnation, The Lover's Bouquet . . .

My mind is filled with colour still;
with each stroke you are there again, my bride
lying on our crimson bed, our wedding night.
Things have changed. You wouldn't like it much.

The green violinist now grumbles
into his prayer book, has retired to an old
people's home in the suburb, refuses
to play me a tune on his purple fiddle.

Lovers no longer fly over fields or church spires,
milk cows in their Sunday best, go to the circus —
but still I keep them alive, the images.
I have been cursed, my love, with long life,

you dead now more than forty summers.
The old grandfather clock has finally stopped,
your absence no longer measured
by its metronome, the slow arm of loss.

I count the silent hours till I give up
the ghost. You stand before me,
again My Fiancée With Black Gloves.
My soul is vivid blue. It will know you.

NOEL DUFFY

I See My Friend Everywhere

First she died   then on the bus
I saw her   my old friend dropped
her half fare into the slot
looked up   her eyes humorous
intelligent   cap of white hair
shining   I asked her   how's the boy
these days   not so good but you
know that   your work   is it going
well?   what work she whispered   (bitterly
I thought)   are you all right?   why
do you ask?   I was afraid of her

the bus rocked and bumped over and
through New York   unsteady   I called out
STOP this is where I get off   here?
since when?   oh for the last couple
of years   she nearly touched my hand
yes   I said   you were still alive

GRACE PALEY

55

A Garage in County Cork

Surely you paused at this roadside oasis
In your nomadic youth, and saw the mound
Of never-used cement, the curious faces,
The soft-drink ads and the uneven ground
Rainbowed with oily puddles, where a snail
Had scrawled its slimy, phosphorescent trail.

Like a frontier store-front in an old western
It might have nothing behind it but thin air,
Building materials, fruit boxes, scrap iron,
Dust-laden shrubs and coils of rusty wire,
A cabbage-white fluttering in the sodden
Silence of an untended kitchen garden —

Nirvana! But the cracked panes reveal a dark
Interior echoing with the cries of children.
Here in this quiet corner of County Cork
A family ate, slept, and watched the rain
Dance clean and cobalt the exhausted grit
So that the mind shrank from the glare of it.

Where did they go? South Boston? Cricklewood?
Somebody somewhere thinks of this as home,
Remembering the old pumps where they stood,
Antique now, squirting juice into a cream
Lagonda or a dung-caked tractor while
A cloud swam on a cloud-reflecting tile.

Surely a white-washed sun-trap at the back
Gave way to hens, wild thyme, and the first few
Shadowy yards of an overgrown cart track,
Tyres in the branches such as Noah knew —
Beyond, a swoop of mountain where you heard,
Disconsolate in the haze, a single blackbird.

Left to itself, the functional will cast
A death-bed glow of picturesque abandon.
The intact antiquities of the recent past,
Dropped from the retail catalogues, return
To the materials that gave rise to them
And shine with a late sacramental gleam.

A god who spent the night here once rewarded
Natural courtesy with eternal life —
Changing to petrol pumps, that they be spared
For ever there, an old man and his wife.
The virgin who escaped his dark design
Sanctions the townland from her prickly shrine.

We might be anywhere but are in one place only,
One of the milestones of earth-residence
Unique in each particular, the thinly
Peopled hinterland serenely tense —
Not in the hope of a resplendent future
But with a sure sense of its intrinsic nature.

Derek Mahon

Logan

When the plane rose into the night
trailing from its great wing
Nantucket, the Cape, and farther in
a massive web of light,
the pilot prompted us to look left
and find the moon in eclipse,
charting our route north and east
along the coast of Maine.

I wondered where you were
and gazed through the porthole
at a star in darkness
and the earth a shadow penny
stuck motionless on the moon's face,
and you down there unknown
to me and vanished in a constellation,
Boston at the edge of water.

CATHERINE PHIL MACCARTHY

Winter Ball

The squat man under the hoop
throws in short hooks, left-handed, right
in the dwindling sunlight as six lesbians
clown and shoot at the other end,
through a very loose game of three on three.

How pleased to be among themselves,
warm New Year's Day afternoon, neither young
nor graceful nor really good shots
but happy for the moment while a mutt
belonging to one of them runs

nearly out of its skin so glad to be
near the action and smells, vigorous and dumb
but keeping his orbits well-clear of the man
who would be a machine now if he could,
angling them in off both sides of the backboard.

You can tell this is a thing he's often done,
the boy who'd shoot till dusk
when starlings exploded, filthy birds
from roost to roost, gathering only to fly off
at the first sharp sound, hundreds as one.

He'd wonder where they went at night
as he played his solitary game of *Round the World*,
sinking shots from along the perimeter,
then the lay-up, then the foul.
                              So intent at it
and grave it almost seemed like more than a game
with dark coming on and the cold.

AUGUST KLEINZAHLER

This Moon, These Stars

Something is changing.
There is a September stillness in the garden.

We have woken in this bed for years.
You have followed me into my poems,
my dreams, my past, to places I scarcely
know of myself.

I called one evening
from our back doorstep. 'Look,' I said,
'look at this moon.' We stood there
in silence, not touching, not knowing
what to say.

We have been together many days, many nights.
These stars have come out
over us again and again.

Here is the life we are living,
not on a windswept beach, not in vast
city streets, not in a strange country
but here, where we have chosen to be.

I look at myself in the glass, at the woman
I am.

I think of our days, our years running on
into each other.

What will we say,
what will we know.
Separate, together,
will we find the right way, the dream
neither of us can explain.

I pull the living room curtains together.
The garden is around us,
still above us are the stars,
light and indestructible.

JOAN MCBREEN

My Father Perceived as a Vision of St Francis

for Brendan Kennelly

It was the piebald horse in next door's garden
frightened me out of a dream
with her dawn whinny. I was back
in the boxroom of the house,
my brother's room now,
full of ties and sweaters and secrets.
Bottles chinked on the doorstep,
the first bus pulled up to the stop.
The rest of the house slept

except for my father. I heard
him rake the ash from the grate,
plug in the kettle, hum a snatch of a tune.
Then he unlocked the back door
and stepped out into the garden.

Autumn was nearly done, the first frost
whitened the slates of the estate.
He was older than I had reckoned,
his hair completely silver,
and for the first time I saw the stoop
of his shoulder, saw that
his leg was stiff. What's he at?
So early and still stars in the west?

They came then: birds
of every size, shape, colour; they came
from the hedges and shrubs,
from eaves and garden sheds,
from the industrial estate, outlying fields,
from Dubber Cross they came
and the ditches of the North Road.

The garden was a pandemonium
when my father threw up his hands
and tossed the crumbs in the air. The sun

cleared O'Reilly's chimney
and he was suddenly radiant,
a perfect vision of St Francis,
made whole, made young again,
in a Finglas garden.

PAULA MEEHAN

It Is Marvellous to Wake Up Together

It is marvellous to wake up together
At the same minute; marvellous to hear
The rain begin suddenly all over the roof,
To feel the air clear
As if electricity had passed through it
From a black mesh of wires in the sky.
All over the roof the rain hisses,
And below, the light falling of kisses.

An electrical storm is coming or moving away;
It is the prickling air that wakes us up.
If lightning struck the house now, it would run
From the four blue china balls on top
Down the roof and down the rods all around us,
and we imagine dreamily
How the whole house caught in a bird-cage of lightning
Would be quite delightful rather than frightening:

And from the same simplified point of view
Of night and lying flat on one's back
All things might change equally easily,
Since always to warn us there must be these black
Electrical wires dangling. Without surprise

The world might change to something quite different,
As the air changes or the lightning comes without our
blinking.
Change as our kisses are changing without our thinking.

ELIZABETH BISHOP

The Wishing Tree

I thought of her as the wishing tree that died
And saw it lifted, root and branch, to heaven,
Trailing a shower of all that had been driven

Need by need by need into its hale
Sap-wood and bark: coin and pin and nail
Came streaming from it like a comet-tail

New-minted and dissolved. I had a vision
Of an airy branch-head rising through damp cloud,
Of turned-up faces where the tree had stood.

SEAMUS HEANEY

May
for Marian

The blessèd stretch and ease of it —
heart's ease. The hills blue. All the flowering weeds
bursting open. Balm in the air. The birdsong
bouncing back out of the sky. The cattle
lain down in the meadow, forgetting to feed.
The horses swishing their tails.
The yellow flare of furze on the near hill.
And the first cream splatters of blossom
high on the thorns where the day rests longest.

All hardship, hunger, treachery of winter
forgotten.
This unfounded conviction: forgiveness, hope.

KERRY HARDIE

For Andrew

'Will I die?' you ask. And so I enter on
The dutiful exposition of that which you
Would rather not know, and I rather not tell you.
To soften my 'Yes' I offer compensations —
Age and fulfilment ('It's so far away;
You will have children and grandchildren by then')
And indifference ('By then you will not care').
No need: you cannot believe me, convinced
That if you always eat plenty of vegetables
And are careful crossing the street you will live for ever.
And so we close the subject, with much unsaid —
This, for instance: Though you and I may die
Tomorrow or next year, and nothing remain
Of our stock, of the unique, preciously-hoarded
Inimitable genes we carry in us,
It is possible that for many generations
There will exist, sprung from whatever seeds,
Children straight-limbed, with clear enquiring voices,
Bright-eyed as you. Or so I like to think:
Sharing in this your childish optimism.

FLEUR ADCOCK

Italy, 1996

This Italian earth is special to me
because I was here in a war
when I was young and immortal.
I remember the cypresses in the early morning light
on the road to the airfield
before the sky filled with toiling planes
massing high over Italy for the perilous
crossing to Germany. I remember
on the way back from the target toasting
my frozen cheese sandwich — frozen by the high
    altitude —
on the electrically-heated casing of my fifty-caliber
machine gun. I remember the taste of life.

HARVEY SHAPIRO

Dark School

It is dusk when I enter the classroom,
the last of the chalky Latin verbs going out on the
    board.
I sit at a desk at the back
and dip my first real pen into blue-black ink.
My jotter is dusty pink.

I rule a margin, one inch wide,
then write the names of the lost, the dead,
in a careful, legible list.
I memorise this, stand up,
recite it word-for-word to twenty shadowy desks.
The tall windows blacken and fill with night.

But I can see in this blurred school,
my carved initials, soft scars on the wood,
and when I open the lid of my desk
there are my books, condition fair,
my difficult lessons.

I must not run in the corridor,
but walk at the speed of smell
to the hall, to the empty stage,
along the silent passageway to the gym
where my hands grasp the hanging rope that brushes my
    face.

Dark school. I learn well; the black paintings
in their burnt frames; all by heart —
the lightless speeches in the library,
the bleak equations, the Greek for darkness.
Above the glass roof of the chemistry lab,
the insolent, truant stars squander their light.

CAROL ANN DUFFY

Sunday Afternoon

In the ordinary house of love
We move quietly from room to room.
Here you are pensive at a window,

Your cheek flat on the green pane,
And the oak outside marks
A corner of silence in a summer room.
Beyond again, in a greater room,
Swallows curl to a punctured ceiling,
And beyond again . . .

And all of my windows open to the fresh wind,
To the gold light refined through your hair.
A knock on the door of childhood

And the walls dissolve in music,
Soft beat of your dancer's foot,
White recession of doorways in your eye.

THEO DORGAN

[An Atlas of the Difficult World]
XIII   (Dedications)

I know you are reading this poem
late, before leaving your office
of the one intense yellow lamp-spot and the darkening
  window
in the lassitude of a building faded to quiet
long after rush-hour.   I know you are reading this poem
standing up in a bookstore far from the ocean
on a grey day of early spring, faint flakes driven
across the plains' enormous spaces around you.
I know you are reading this poem
in a room where too much has happened for you to bear
where the bedclothes lie in stagnant coils on the bed
and the open valise speaks of flight
but you cannot leave yet.   I know you are reading this
  poem
as the underground train loses momentum and before
  running up the stairs
toward a new kind of love
your life has never allowed.
I know you are reading this poem by the light
of the television screen where soundless images jerk and
  slide
while you wait for the newscast from the *intifada*.
I know you are reading this poem in a waiting-room
of eyes met and unmeeting, of identity with strangers.

I know you are reading this poem by fluorescent light
in the boredom and fatigue of the young who are
    counted out,
count themselves out, at too early an age.   I know
you are reading this poem through your failing sight, the
    thick
lens enlarging these letters beyond all meaning yet you
    read on
because even the alphabet is precious.
I know you are reading this poem as you pace beside the
    stove
warming milk, a crying child on your shoulder, a book in
    your hand
because life is short and you too are thirsty.
I know you are reading this poem which is not in your
    language
guessing at some words while others keep you reading
and I want to know which words they are.
I know you are reading this poem listening for something,
    torn between bitterness and hope
turning back once again to the task you cannot refuse.
I know you are reading this poem because there is
    nothing else left to read
there where you have landed, stripped as you are.

ADRIENNE RICH

In Memory of Alois Alzheimer
(1864 – 1915)

I

Before this page fades from memory,
spare a thought for Alois Alzheimer,
called to mind each time

someone becomes forgetful,
disintegration vindicating
his good name.

II

His is the last image assigned
to the ex-President who has slipped
from public view; soiled sheets
give credence to his thesis;

his territory is marked out
by the track of urine
dribbled along the corridor
of the day-care centre.

III

Lie closer to me in the dry sheets
while I can still tell who you are.

Let me declare how much I love you
before our bed is sorely tested.

Love me with drooling toxins, with carbon monoxide,
with rope, with arrows through my heart.

DENNIS O'DRISCOLL

When All Is Said and Done

what I wanted
was

to marry young

have children
and more children

dance and act up a storm

have a husband's love
that would never end

die last of my family

how was I to know
I would be my own woman at last

without all that

LUCY BRENNAN

Fireman's Lift

I was standing beside you looking up
Through the big tree of the cupola
Where the church splits wide open to admit
Celestial choirs, the fall-out of brightness.

The Virgin was spiralling to heaven,
Hauled up in stages. Past mist and shining,
Teams of angelic arms were heaving,
Supporting, crowding her, and we stepped

Back, as the painter longed to
While his arm swept in the large strokes.
We saw the work entire, and how the light

Melted and faded bodies so that
Loose feet and elbows and staring eyes
Floated in the wide stone petticoat
Clear and free as weeds.

This is what love sees, that angle:
The crick in the branch loaded with fruit,
A jaw defining itself, a shoulder yoked,

The back making itself a roof
The legs a bridge, the hands
A crane and a cradle.

Their heads bowed over to reflect on her
Fair face and hair so like their own
As she passed through their hands. We saw them
Lifting her, the pillars of their arms

(Her face a capital leaning into an arch)
As the muscles clung and shifted
For a final purchase together
Under her weight as she came to the edge of the cloud.

Eiléan Ní Chuilleanáin

Autumn Song

Autumn returns, and again the trees
shed volumes, all of them seeming
to whisper the same word: sleep.

It would be very easy now to sleep
and not to wake again, to lie
in the quiet of this city flat

like an old toy or a bloodstain
and let days creep past. It would be
no negation of the light that's been

to accept the dark's embrace and turn
into myself. And yet last year,
though the leaves eventually turned to pulp

and rain and snow transformed the street,
then vanished, one day I woke to see
a beam of light from this high window

probe the corners, sweep the room,
a beam I felt myself drawn towards
as a seed must feel itself drawn back

into the world.

PAT BORAN

Eden Rock

They are waiting for me somewhere beyond Eden Rock:
My father, twenty-five, in the same suit
Of Genuine Irish Tweed, his terrier Jack
Still two years old and trembling at his feet.

My mother, twenty-three, in a sprigged dress
Drawn at the waist, ribbon in her straw hat,
Has spread the stiff white cloth over the grass.
Her hair, the colour of wheat, takes on the light.

She pours tea from a Thermos, the milk straight
From an old HP sauce bottle, a screw
Of paper for a cork; slowly sets out
The same three plates, the tin cups painted blue.

The sky whitens as if lit by three suns.
My mother shades her eyes and looks my way
Over the drifted stream. My father spins
A stone along the water. Leisurely,

They beckon to me from the other bank.
I hear them call, 'See where the stream-path is!
Crossing is not as hard as you might think.'

I had not thought that it would be like this.

CHARLES CAUSLEY

Lovebirds

So she moved into the hospital the last nine days
to tend him with little strokes and murmurs
as he sank into the sheets. Nurse
set out a low bed for her, night-times, next to his.
He nuzzled up to her as she brushed
away the multiplying cells with a sigh,
was glad as she ignored the many
effluents and the tang of death. The second
last morning of his life he opened
his eyes, saying, 'I can't wake up'
but wouldn't close them for his nap
until he was sure she was there.
Later he moved quietly to deeper sleep.
as Professor said he would, still listening
to her twittering on and on until the last.

JO SHAPCOTT

Parents

A child's face is a drowned face:
Her parents stare down at her asleep
Estranged from her by a sea:
She is under the sea
And they are above the sea:
If she looked up she would see them
As if locked out of their own home,
Their mouths open,
Their foreheads furrowed —
Pursed-up orifices of fearful fish —
Their big ears are fins behind glass
And in her sleep she is calling out to them
    Father, Father
    Mother, Mother
But they cannot hear her:
She is inside the sea
And they are outside the sea.
Through the night, stranded, they stare
At the drowned, drowned face of their child.

PAUL DURCAN

Mother

There is a room in my head, to which you often come
orchid gifts wet with rain in one hand —
in the other, your love
wrapped up in a cut-out newspaper piece
you'd saved just for me
or maybe sealed tight in irregular pots
of home-made orange jam.

You come in and we quickly leave behind
the thorny rose-gardens of our grown-up fights.
I smooth out the creases in your gentle face
I know I've often caused —
while you, keeping me from the shabby coldness
of this outside world,
put the last stitch on my coat.

ENDA WYLEY

In the Attic

Even though we know now
your clothes will never
be needed, we keep them,
upstairs in a locked trunk.

Sometimes I kneel there,
touching them, trying to relive
time you wore them, to remember
the actual shape of arm and wrist.

My hands push down
between hollow, invisible sleeves,
hesitate, then take hold
and lift:

a green holiday; a red christening;
all your unfinished lives
fading through dark summers
entering my head as dust.

ANDREW MOTION

Pad, Pad

I always remember your beautiful flowers
And the beautiful kimono you wore
When you sat on the couch
With that tigerish crouch
And told me you loved me no more.

What I cannot remember is how I felt when you were
 unkind
All I know is, if you were unkind now I should not
 mind.
Ah me, the power to feel exaggerated, angry and sad
The years have taken from me. Softly I go now, pad pad.

STEVIE SMITH

Keeping Pacific Time

The last class over,
You are walking to your car now;

And your day winds down,
A penny spun on a table.

Gravel and crushed grass sigh
Where the night wind crosses them,

For the warm rubbish of picnics,
Toddlers held among bushes;

And the park, policed at nightfall,
Privately dreams of children

While the statues throw their arms
To a sky refusing pigeons:

Many white faces,
Longhaired in the moonlight.

On the other side of the world
Where I live, missing you,

It is early morning. Light
Collects like rain in the awnings.

Dew on the closed newsstands,
And the first bread cooling.

Soon the crows will come,
Just as they do at home

To the trellis sloped like Pisa,
For the crumbs on my window:

A scone broken in bits,
And softened under the cold tap.

AIDAN MATHEWS

Over and Over

Over and over they suffer, the gentle creatures,
The frightened deer, the mice in the corn to be gathered,
Over and over we cry, alone or together.
And we weep for a lot we scarcely understand,
Wondering why we are here and what we mean
And why there are huge stars and volcanic eruptions,
Earthquakes, desperate disasters of many kinds.
What is the answer? Is there

One? There are many. Most of us forget
The times when the going sun was a blaze of gold
And the blue hung behind it and we were the whole of
    awe,
We forget the moments of love and cast out time
And the children who come to us trusting the answers
    we give
To their difficult and important questions. And there

Are shooting stars and rainbows and broad blue seas.
Surely when we gather the good about us
The dark is cancelled out. Mysteries must
Be our way of life. Without them we might
Stop trying to learn and hoping to succeed
In the work we half-choose and giving the love we need.

ELIZABETH JENNINGS

A Garden on the Point

Now it is Easter and the speckled bean
Breaks open underground, the liquid snail
Winces and waits, trapped on the lawn's light green;
The burdened clothes-line heaves and barks in the gale,
And lost in flowers near the garage wall
Child and mother fumble, tidy, restrain.

And now great ebb tides lift to the light of day
The sea-bed's briny chambers of decay.

THOMAS KINSELLA

Ladies Waiting Room, Thurles Station

Cool as a milk-churn, bare as a mountain field,
A smoulder of sods in the grate, that winter scent —
Before I came to know her, this room did; the chair,
The butter-coloured walls, the grey wainscotting. Her
Coty powder perfumed its air for an hour —
A voice complains outside; a delay at the Junction —
And Blackie neighs in the station-yard as my ghostly
Grandfather gives him the nod. Now they've gone.

She was a girl in a red coat going back to Dublin.
Some stranger maybe combing her hair half-saw
That precious face in the mirror and remarked
The train was late. My mother, I imagine, agreed;
Politely, absently, as she often did . . . Briefly, I am she.
But what else she said, or really thought, is lost to me.

ANNE HAVERTY

The Empty House

When we are gone, the house will close over us
as though we'd been swimmers in an unmoved sea.
The cisterns will unruffle, the fridge will wheeze on,
and the shape we made in the bed will pucker out.

The house will replace us with sounds of its own:
the shuffle of pages as we pull the door hard,
the phone ringing out, the occasional clock,
and only the letterbox will break the settled air.

All these shadows from the beech tree in the back
that close on my arm as I reach to turn the key
will swell with a glitter that will take in the room
and, this evening, drain what is left of us away.

VONA GROARKE

Alla Luna
a lunar cycle

Last summer
we lived
on the planet
of purest sadness
looking at people
in the streets
like aliens —
looking at each day
as if it were the last.
We spoke to the moon
without words,
without hope.

*

There was a blue pool
in the sky.
We liked swimming
up there when the moon
and some stars
floated in the water.
You had to be careful
not to butterfly
through a cloud
or dog paddle
into the universe.

*

What was the deal last summer?
We were surrounded
by sky in all directions.
If it wasn't dawn over the lake
it was dusk over the buildings.
Not to mention lightning,
orbiting sky furniture
like stars, planets,
then examining the moon
through your telescope.
All we ever did
was try to sit still
holding our breath
watching the heavens
for a sign.

*

Oh really —
let's all gaze at the moon
and have a nervous breakdown
since life stinks.
I was looking at the lake sideways,
my head on a pillow
wishing and wishing
you would get better.
The moon went blurry:
space-garbage sneering
at me and my sadness.

*

A year ago
I stood at the window
high in the sky crying.
I focused my father's telescope,
saw lunar mountains, craters, valleys.
'Well, moon,' I said,
'How can I ever be happy again
when my father is disappearing
to a place I can't visualise?'
Luna, I watched you change
all summer into a harvest moon
just before he died.

*

If you were still
in this solar system
we'd be e-mailing
comet sightings
to each other like crazy
and you'd have flipped
watching Hale-Bopp
through your skyscraper windows
on Sheridan Road.
But now I guess
you're some kind of asteroid yourself
travelling to wherever.
Great timing, Jack.
You're missing everything.

JULIE O'CALLAGHAN

November

We walk to the ward from the badly parked car
with your grandma taking four short steps to our two.
We have brought her here to die and we know it.

You check her towel, soap and family trinkets,
pare her nails, parcel her in the rough blankets
and she sinks down into her incontinence.

It is time John. In their pasty bloodless smiles,
in their slack breasts, their stunned brains and their
    baldness,
and in us John: we are almost these monsters.

You're shattered. You give me the keys and I drive
through the twilight zone, past the famous station
to your house, to numb ourselves with alcohol.

Inside, we feel the terror of dusk begin.
Outside we watch the evening, failing again,
and we let it happen. We can say nothing.

Sometimes the sun spangles and we feel alive.
One thing we have to get, John, out of this life.

SIMON ARMITAGE

Snow at the Opera House

They're serving coffee in the marbled hall.
At the other end, glass balcony doors
reflect the chandeliers, the vast mirrors
in golden frames. Beyond, it's night. The snow
falls. Light spills over the parapet
and out there, four lamps cast an aura
that shows every flake, tumbling, in perfect
rhythm with the rest, into the lighted arc,
then out of it again, fading back
into darkness to blend with all the others
and finally, settle. I rest
my forehead on the cold of the window-pane
and clasp my cup. It warms me through the woollen
gloves and for a short while, this is more
than just one person, heavy with dampness
seeping through boots and too many sweaters,
that as well but getting ready not to be,
with the brightness of the snow, the soft dark
of the night out there, the scent of coffee, the A
that's gathering in from the discord of strings
and flutes and the rest, calling us together,
and in the few minutes that it takes to finish
my coffee, all this is contained. And the snow
falling, falling.
I will never forget it.
Now, it's not quite spring and the snow is long gone
but something of its quality remains:

an awareness, of moments
as separate
like snowflakes that fall,
gather, settle into something else
and seem to disappear.

LIZ MCSKEANE

The Chinese Restaurant in Portrush

Before the first visitor comes the spring
Softening the sharp air of the coast
In time for the first seasonal 'invasion'.
Today the place is as it might have been,
Gentle and almost hospitable. A girl
Strides past the Northern Counties Hotel,
Light-footed, swinging a book-bag,
And the doors that were shut all winter
Against the north wind and the sea-mist
Lie open to the street, where one
By one the gulls go window-shopping
And an old wolfhound dozes in the sun.

While I sit with my paper and prawn chow mein
Under a framed photograph of Hong Kong
The proprietor of the Chinese restaurant
Stands at the door as if the world were young,
Watching the first yacht hoist a sail
  — An ideogram on sea-cloud — and the light
Of heaven upon the hills of Donegal;
And whistles a little tune, dreaming of home.

DEREK MAHON

Seatown

Sanctuary of sorts for the herons all day yesterday
waiting for the estuary to drain and this evening
for two lights queuing like crystal at the top of the bay.

Last straw for the panel beaters only just closed down
and the dole office next to the barracks and the gold
of beer spilled on the pavements of Saturday afternoon.

Home from home for the likes of us and foreign boats
and groups with oilskins and unheard-of currencies
in search of common ground and teenage prostitutes.

Reclaimed ward of bins left out a week and dogs in heat
and the fragrance of salt and sewage that bleeds
into our garden from the neap-tide of an August night.

Poor man's Latin Quarter of stevedores and an early
house
and three huge silos swamped by the small hours
and the buzz of joyriders quite close on the bypass.

Time of life to settle for making a fist of love
and glimpsing new dawns and being caught again
and waking in waves with all the sheets kicked off.

Point of no return for the cattle feed on the wharves
and the old shoreline and the windmill without sails
and time that keeps for no one, least of all ourselves.

May its name be said for as long as it could matter.
Or, failing that, for as long as it takes the pilot
to negotiate the eight kilometres from this to open
water.

CONOR O'CALLAGHAN

On a Son Returned to New Zealand

He is my green branch growing in a far plantation.
He is my first invention.

No one can be in two places at once.
So we left Athens on the same morning.
I was in a hot railway carriage, crammed
between Serbian soldiers and peasant
women, on sticky seats, with nothing to
drink but warm mineral water.
                                        He was
in a cabin with square windows, sailing
across the Mediterranean, fast,
to Suez.
            Then I was back in London
in the tarnished summer, remembering,
as I folded his bed up, and sent the
television set away. Letters came
from Aden and Singapore, late.
                                        He was
already in his father's house, on the
cliff-top, where the winter storms roll across
from Kapiti Island, and the flax bends
before the wind. He could go no further.

He is my bright sea-bird on a rocky beach.

FLEUR ADCOCK

She Replies to Carmel's Letter

It was a mild Christmas, the small fine rain kept washing
    over,
so I coated myself in plastics,
walked further than I could manage.
Leave me now, I'd say, and when they had tramped ahead
I'd sit myself down on a stone or the side of a high grass
    ditch,
or anywhere — like a duck in a puddle —
I'd rest a bit, then I would muddle around
the winding boreens that crawled the headland.

Sometimes, water-proofed and not caring,
I'd sit in a road which was really a stream-bed,
being and seeing from down where the hare sees,
sitting in mud and in wetness,
the world rising hummocky round me,
the sudden grass on the skyline,
the fence-post, with the earth run from under it,
swinging like a hanged man.

Then I would want to praise

the ease of low wet things, the song of them, like a
    child's low drone,

and praising I'd watch how the water flowing the track

is clear, so I might not see it

but for the cross-hatched place where it runs on a
    scatter of grit,

the flat, swelled place where it slides itself over a stone.

So now, when you write that you labour to strip off the
    layers,

and there might not, under them, be anything at all,

I remember that time, and I wish you had sat there, with
    me,

your skin fever-hot, the lovely wet coldness of winter
    mud

on your red, uncovered hands,

knowing it's all in the layers,

the flesh on the bones, the patterns that the bones push

upwards onto the flesh. So, you will see how it is with
    me,

and that sometimes even sickness is generous

and takes you by the hand and sits you

beside things you would otherwise have passed over.

KERRY HARDIE

He Leaves the Ironing Board Open

He likes
crisp white shirts
and Tracy Chapman.
He leaves
the ironing board open
in his mobile home
near the motorway,
so that he is halfway there
if he ever makes the decision
to go out.

He plays
Tracy Chapman
really loud
in his mobile home
near the motorway,
so that he can't hear
the noise of the cars
or the screech of his loneliness
crashing into him
from every side.

RITA ANN HIGGINS

The Way My Mother Speaks

I say her phrases to myself
in my head
or under the shallows of my breath,
restful shapes moving.
The day and ever. The day and ever.

The train this slow evening
goes down England
browsing for the right sky,
too blue swapped for a cool grey.
For miles I have been saying
What like is it
the way I say things when I think.
Nothing is silent. Nothing is not silent.
What like is it.

Only tonight
I am happy and sad
like a child
who stood at the end of summer
and dipped a net
in a green, erotic pond. *The day
and ever. The day and ever.*
I am homesick, free, in love
with the way my mother speaks.

Carol Ann Duffy

The Trees

The trees are coming into leaf
Like something almost being said;
The recent buds relax and spread,
Their greenness is a kind of grief.

Is it that they are born again
And we grow old? No, they die too.
Their yearly trick of looking new
Is written down in rings of grain.

Yet still the unresting castles thresh
In fullgrown thickness every May.
Last year is dead, they seem to say,
Begin afresh, afresh, afresh.

PHILIP LARKIN

Finale

The cruellest thing they did
was to send home his teeth from the hospital.

What could she do with those,
arriving as they did days after the funeral?

Wrapped them in one of his clean handkerchiefs
she'd laundered and taken down.
All she could do was cradle them in her hands;
they looked so strange, alone —

utterly jawless in a constant smile
not in the least like his. She could cry no more.
At midnight she took heart and aim and threw
them out of the kitchen door.

It rocketed out, that finally-parted smile,
into the gully? the scrub? the neighbour's land?
And she went back and fell into stupid sleep,
knowing him dead at last, and by her hand.

JUDITH WRIGHT

Hedgehog

The snail moves like a
Hovercraft, held up by a
Rubber cushion of itself,
Sharing its secret

With the hedgehog. The hedgehog
Shares its secret with no one.
We say, *Hedgehog, come out*
Of yourself and we will love you.

We mean no harm. We want
Only to listen to what
You have to say. We want
Your answers to our questions.

The hedgehog gives nothing
Away, keeping itself to itself.
We wonder what a hedgehog
Has to hide, why it so distrusts.

We forget the god
Under this crown of thorns.
We forget that never again
Will a god trust in the world.

Paul Muldoon

Broken Moon
for Emma

Twelve, small as six,
strength, movement, hearing,
all given in half measure,
my daughter,
child of genetic carelessness,
walks uphill, always.

I watch her morning face;
precocious patience as she hooks each sock,
creeps it up her foot,
aims her jersey like a quoit.
My fingers twitch;
her private frown deters.

Her jokes can sting:
'My life is like dressed crab
 — lot of effort, rather little meat.'
Yet she delights in seedlings taking root,
finding a fossil,
a surprise dessert.

Chopin will not yield to her stiff touch;
I hear her cursing.
She paces Bach exactly,
firm rounding of perfect cadences.
Somewhere inside
she is dancing a courante.

In dreams she skims the sand,
curls toes into the ooze of pools,
leaps on to stanchions.
Awake, her cousins take her hands;
they lean into the waves,
stick-child between curved sturdiness.

She turns away from stares,
laughs at the boy who asks
if she will find a midget husband.
Ten years ago, cradling her,
I showed her the slice of silver in the sky.
'Moon broken', she said.

CAROL SATYAMURTI

The Great Stretch

At the doors of red-brick
houses in a narrow street,
women are proclaiming
a great stretch in the evenings!

I've been away,
skating on the full rink of the world,
and return to find them
still speaking the mysteries

of made beds that must be lain upon,
of roses, thorns, and money not
growing on trees, but above all
of this wonderful lengthening of day.

Above our heads, seagulls, swallows
test the new elasticity of the sky.

Through such reluctant twilight
these women chased us home
on summer nights, threatening
the sandman, the bogeyman . . .

they linger, basking in protracted light.

KATHERINE DUFFY

Beach Café: Portugal

Stately on mopeds, the lovers
leave to do their homework.
An ambulance mourns along the avenue
and shadows run like spilled wine
beside the empty chairs.
A fat woman, crippled,
crochets perfect dreams,
drawing a long white thread
as the tide turns.
The waiter rests on his shield.
At last you can hear the sea
inhale, exhale.

JOHN WAKEMAN

Old People

Wet mouths in dark rooms, old people wait
for a kiss, for a mole on a cheek
to brush your cheek, for you to fall
over their feet splayed out in ancient slippers,
their thick, brown-stockinged, knobbled legs.
Low in overblown floral chairs, they sit
with their enormous khaki handkerchiefs,
dabbing at something.

Old people: they live alone, their green bakelite clocks
tick loud through anything you say, you can't ignore
the patterns on their walls, that tyranny of roses
marching your eye on a meaningless pilgrimage,
again and again and again. They drink brown drinks
from glasses filmy as their eyes; they want you to hold
    them,
their hands are ready, loose skin, brown spots,
the slippery veins.

Old people, there's always a ball of wool coming from
    them,
they knit and knit and knit, do darning with mushrooms,
embroider cushions, put smocking on dresses;
they cry in chairs. They leave themselves about in pieces —
three pairs of glasses, three hard snappy cases,
mugs of livid gums with teeth — you look for things
you half-expect to find and know you shouldn't;
you don't know what stays in.

Old people want you to hold them together.
They lie in bed and smile and watch
your shaking fingers plait their hair.

CHRISTINA DUNHILL

Parting

Darling, this is goodbye. The words are ordinary
But love is rare. So let it go tenderly
as the sound of violins into silence.

Parting is sad for us, because something is over.
But for the thing we have ended, it is a beginning —
Let love go like a young bird flying from the nest.

Like a new star, airborne into the evening.
Watched out of sight, or let fall gently as a tear.
Let our love go out of the world, like the prayer for a
  soul's rest.

Let the roses go, that you fastened in my hair
One summer night in a garden, and the song
That we heard from another house, where a piano was
  playing:
The shadow a street lamp cast through the net of a
  curtain.
The river at night, smooth and silent Thames, flowing
  through London.

For two years Ullswater was silver with my love of you
The golden birch-leaves were holy, the wild cherry was
    sweet
On the fell-sides, scenting the spring for you.
The bees, drunk with the lime-flowers, dropped like
    grapes on the road.
And the silence was yours, over all Westmorland at
    night.

I raised the mountains for you, and set the streams
Running down the hills for love. I saw the moss grow
And the ferns unroll their croziers for love of you,
The snowdrops, the primrose, the heron, the martin,
    the sheep on the fells.

The snow was yours in winter, and the frost crystals
That shone like amethyst and sapphire in the starlight,
That grew their geometric beauty on the trees' animate
    branches.
The frozen waterfall, the coral caves of ice,
The noise of water rushing from the thawing springs.

The wind on the mountain, the shelter of the garden,
The stone seat under the yew-tree, the fire in the
    evening,
Home-baked loaves, and apples, trout from the beck
I loved for you, held holy for you, my darling.

That was erotic. That was one with the grass,
One with the night, the animals and the stars.
All that is mortal in us, and must pass,
Creatures whose own death is their unguessed secret,
Loving in one another the rose that must fade.

Yours, too, was the anteroom of the angels,
When I could hear a pin drop, or a drop of rain,
Or the creak of a beam, or the butterfly caught in the
    rafters.
I wrestled with angels for you, and in my body
Endured the entire blessing of love's pain.

All this is true. These things, my dear, are a life
Lived for love of you. The fire in my heart, the fire on
    the hearth,
And children's stories in the evening, even hope's death
Were precious for you. Precious all things in time
And outside time. The poem I know, and the wisdom
That is not mine, the poem that can never be written.

To you, one man among all men, I dedicate
The world I have known, my days and nights, my
    flowers,
The angels, the sorrows, the forms of life I consecrate
In your name, far beyond ourselves, or any selves —
These attributes are God's.

To you, once loved and for ever, from whom I part
Not because fate is blind, or the heart cold,
But because the world is neither yours nor mine,
Not even ourselves, not even what is dearest,
I offer what I can, my living moment,
My human span.

KATHLEEN RAINE

Reading Pascal in the Lowlands

His aunt has gone astray in her concern
And the boy's mum leans across his wheelchair
To talk to him. She points to the river.
An aged angler and a boy they know
Cast lazily into the rippled sun.
They go there, into the dappled grass, shadows
Bickering and falling from the shaken leaves.

His father keeps apart from them, walking
On the beautiful grass that is bright green
In the sunlight of July at 7 pm.
He sits on the bench beside me, saying
It is a lovely evening, and I rise
From my sorrows, agreeing with him.
His large hand picks tobacco from a tin;

His smile falls at my feet, on the baked earth.
Shoes have shuffled over, and ungrassed.
It is discourteous to ask about
Accidents, or of the sick, the unfortunate.
I do not need to, for he says 'Leukaemia'.
We look at the river, his son holding a rod,
The line going downstream in a cloud of flies.

I close my book, the *Pensées* of Pascal.
I am light with meditation, religiose
And mystic with a day of solitude.
I do not tell him of my own sorrows.
He is bored with misery and premonition.
He has seen the limits of time, asking 'Why?'
Nature is silent on that question.

A swing squeaks in the distance. Runners jog
Round the perimeter. He is indiscreet.
His son is eight years old, with months to live.
His right hand trembles on his cigarette.
He sees my book and then he looks at me,
Knowing me for a stranger. I have said
I am sorry. What more is there to say?

He is called over to the riverbank.
I go away, leaving the Park, walking through
The Golf Course, and then a wood, climbing,
And then bracken and gorse, sheep pasturage.
From a panoptic hill I look down on
A little town, its estuary, its bridge,
Its houses, churches, its undramatic streets.

Douglas Dunn

The Sundial

Owain was ill today. In the night
He was delirious, shouting of lions
In the sleepless heat. Today, dry
And pale, he took a paper circle,
Laid it on the grass which held it
With curling fingers. In the still
Centre he pushed the broken bean
Stick, gathering twelve fragments
Of stone, placed them at measured
Distances. Then he crouched, slightly
Trembling with fever, calculating
The mathematics of sunshine.

He looked up, his eyes dark,
Intelligently adult as though
The wave of fever taught silence
And immobility for the first time.
Here, in his enforced rest, he found
Deliberation, and the slow finger
Of light, quieter than night lions,
More worthy of his concentration.
All day he told the time to me.
All day we felt and watched the sun
Caged in its white diurnal heat
Pointing at us with its black stick.

GILLIAN CLARKE

A Young Woman with a Child on Each Hand

A young woman with a child on each hand
turns at the zebra crossing
to join two more young women,
one pregnant, one tilting a pram.
She is vital, almost beautiful.
Her sons are sturdy and neat.
She walks into the life I am leaving.

When she greets her friends, I am aware
mothercraft has blinded her, till anxiety
thins her voice. I want to call out,
that for her, now is filled

with simple certainties — a spilled cup,
a rowdy room, a bed-time story. But
as she moves down the street, I can
only guess the weight
of her sacrifice, her tenderness
as her hands keep emptying, emptying . . .

ANGELA GREENE

Elegy for a Stillborn Child

I

Your mother walks light as an empty creel
Unlearning the intimate nudge and pull

Your trussed-up weight of seed-flesh and bone-curd
Had insisted on. That evicted world

Contracts round its history, its scar.
Doomsday struck when your collapsed sphere

Extinguished itself in our atmosphere,
Your mother heavy with the lightness in her.

II

For six months you stayed cartographer
Charting my friend from husband towards father.

He guessed a globe behind your steady mound.
Then the pole fell, shooting star, into the ground.

III

On lonely journeys I think of it all,
Birth of death, exhumation for burial,

A wreath of small clothes, a memorial pram,
And parents reaching for a phantom limb.

I drive by remote control on this bare road
Under a drizzling sky, a circling rook,

Past mountain fields, full to the brim with cloud,
White waves riding home on a wintry lough.

SEAMUS HEANEY

As the Rooks Are

Alone as the rooks are
In their high, shaking homes in the sky at the mercy of
    winds,
Alone as the lurking trout or the owl which hoots
Comfortingly. I have a well-crammed mind
And I have deep-down healthy and tough roots

But in this house where I live
In one big room, there is much solitude,
Solitude which can turn to loneliness if
I let it infect me with its darkening mood.
Away from here I have an abundant life,
Friends, love, acclaim and these are good.

And I have imagination
Which can travel me over mountains and rough seas;
I also have the gift of discrimination
High in a house which looks over many trees
I collect sunsets and stars which are now a passion.
And I wave my hand to thousands of lives like this,
But will open my window in winter for conversation.

ELIZABETH JENNINGS

Westering Home

Though you'd be pressed to say exactly where
It first sets in, driving west through Wales
Things start to feel like Ireland. It can't be
The chapels with their clear grey windows,
Or the buzzards menacing the scooped valleys.
In April, have the blurred blackthorn hedges
Something to do with it? Or possibly
The motorway, which seems to lose its nerve
Mile by mile. The houses, up to a point,
With their masoned gables, each upper window
A raised eyebrow. More, though, than all of this,
It's the architecture of the spirit;
The old thin ache you thought that you'd forgotten —
More smoke, admittedly, than flame;
Less tears than rain. And the whole business
Neither here nor there and therefore home.

BERNARD O'DONOGHUE

What Are Years?

What is our innocence,
what is our guilt? All are
    naked, none is safe. And whence
is courage: the unanswered question,
the resolute doubt, —
dumbly calling, deafly listening — that
in misfortune, even death,
    encourages others
    and in its defeat, stirs

    the soul to be strong? He
sees deep and is glad, who
    accedes to mortality
and in his imprisonment rises
upon himself as
the sea in a chasm, struggling to be
free and unable to be,
    in its surrendering
    finds its continuing.

    So he who strongly feels,
behaves. The very bird,
    grown taller as he sings, steels
his form straight up. Though he is captive,
his mighty singing
says, satisfaction is a lowly
thing, how pure a thing is joy.
    This is mortality,
    this is eternity.

MARIANNE MOORE

House Contents

In the disco of a town hotel
boxes are numbered and packed
according to the condition
of their random artefacts.

Wedding gifts from the '30s,
souvenirs from children's trips,
a gilt-framed oil, an inlaid chair,
cut glass and china (chipped).

Objects without purpose,
details adrift from plot:
the piano and piano stool
for sale in separate lots.

VONA GROARKE

Spring Race
for Chris

The chestnuts have it.
One before all the rest
in that line of twelve
where the road swings by Foley's farm
has hitched limp green rags
to every spiked twig it owns

and the rags lift,
thicken in moist light,
fan upon fan. Translucent
as new ghosts, they own no shade.
Beyond, the spread corduroy of spring ploughing.
And lambs shouting into the morning.

KERRY HARDIE

A Summer Night
to Geoffrey Hoyland

Out on the lawn I lie in bed,
Vega conspicuous overhead
    In the windless nights of June,
As congregated leaves complete
Their day's activity; my feet
    Point to the rising moon.

Lucky, this point in time and space
Is chosen as my working-place,
    Where the sexy airs of summer,
The bathing hours and the bare arms,
The leisured drives through a land of farms
    Are good to a newcomer.

Equal with colleagues in a ring
I sit on each calm evening
    Enchanted as the flowers
The opening light draws out of hiding
With all its gradual dove-like pleading,
    Its logic and its powers:

Then later we, though parted then,
May still recall these evenings when
      Fear gave his watch no look;
The lion griefs loped from the shade
And on our knees their muzzles laid,
      And Death put down his book.

Now north and south and east and west
Those I love lie down to rest;
      The moon looks on them all,
The healers and the brilliant talkers
The eccentrics and the silent walkers,
      The dumpy and the tall.

She climbs the European sky,
Churches and power-stations lie
      Alike among earth's fixtures:
Into the galleries she peers
And blankly as a butcher stares
      Upon the marvellous pictures.

To gravity attentive, she
Can notice nothing here, though we
      Whom hunger does not move,
From gardens where we feel secure
Look up and with a sigh endure
      The tyrannies of love:

And, gentle, do not care to know,
Where Poland draws her eastern bow,
    What violence is done,
Nor ask what doubtful act allows
Our freedom in this English house,
    Our picnics in the sun.

Soon, soon, through dykes of our content
The crumpling flood will force a rent
    And, taller than a tree,
Hold sudden death before our eyes
Whose river dreams long hid the size
    And vigours of the sea.

But when the waters make retreat
And through the black mud first the wheat
    In shy green stalks appears,
When stranded monsters gasping lie,
And sounds of riveting terrify
    Their whorled unsubtle ears,

May these delights we dread to lose,
This privacy, need no excuse
    But to that strength belong,
As through a child's rash happy cries
The drowned parental voices rise
    In unlamenting song.

After discharges of alarm
All unpredicted let them calm
   The pulse of nervous nations,
Forgive the murderer in his glass
Tough in their patience to surpass
   The tigress her swift motions.

W. H. AUDEN

A Prayer

In our country they are desecrating churches.
May the rain that pours in pour into the font.
Because no snowflake ever falls in the wrong place,
May snow lie on the altar like an altar cloth.

MICHAEL LONGLEY

Saturday

I am sitting on the step
drinking coffee and
smoking, listening to jazz.
The smoke separates
two scents: fresh paint in the house
behind me; in front,
buddleia.
        The neighbours cut
back our lilac tree —
it shaded their neat garden.
The buddleia will
be next, no doubt; but bees and
all those butterflies
approve of our shaggy trees.

                *

I am painting the front door
with such thick juicy
paint I could almost eat it.
People going past
with their shopping stare at my
bare legs and old shirt.
The door will be sea-green.
              Our
black cat walked across
the painted step and left a
delicate paw-trail.
I swore at her and frightened

two little girls — this
street is given to children.

The other cat is younger,
white and tabby, fat,
with a hoarse voice. In summer
she sleeps all day long
in the rosebay willow-herb,
to lazy to walk
on paint.
        Andrew is upstairs;
having discovered
quick-drying non-drip gloss, he
is old enough now
to paint all his furniture
tangerine and the
woodwork green; he is singing.

*

I am lying in the sun,
in the garden. Bees
dive on white clover beside
my ears. The sky is
Greek blue, with a vapour-trail
chalked right across it.
My transistor radio
talks about the moon.

*

I am floating in the sky.
Below me the house
crouches among its trees like
a cat in long grass.
I want to stroke its roof-ridge
but I think I can
already hear it purring.

FLEUR ADCOCK

Book Ends

I

Baked the day she suddenly dropped dead
we chew it slowly that last apple pie.

Shocked into sleeplessness you're scared of bed.
We never could talk much, and now don't try.

You're like book ends, the pair of you, she'd say,
Hog that grate, say nothing, sit, sleep, stare . . .

The 'scholar' me, you, worn out on poor pay,
only our silence made us seem a pair.

Not as good for staring in, blue gas,
too regular each bud, each yellow spike.

A night you need my company to pass
and she not here to tell us we're alike!

Your life's all shattered into smithereens.

Back in our silences and sullen looks,
for all the Scotch we drink, what's still between 's
not the thirty or so years, but books, books, books.

II

The stone's too full. The wording must be terse.
There's scarcely room to carve the FLORENCE on it —

Come on, it's not as if we're wanting verse.
It's not as if we're wanting a whole sonnet!

After tumblers of neat *Johnny Walker*
(I think that both of us we're on our third)
you said you'd always been a clumsy talker
and couldn't find another, shorter word
for 'beloved' or for 'wife' in the inscription,
but not too clumsy that you can't still cut:

You're supposed to be the bright boy at description
and you can't tell them what the fuck to put!

I've got to find the right words on my own.

I've got the envelope that he'd been scrawling,
mis-spelt, mawkish, stylistically appalling
but I can't squeeze more love into their stone.

TONY HARRISON

Love Song

All four of us out on the doorstep
under the stars. The moon
its intense sidelong glance
still two days from full.
Barefoot, the cool
after days of stonebreaking heat.

You sing a wonderful
Spanish love song:
I love you in the morning,
I love you in the afternoon,
I love you under the moon.

In the distance
at the end of our street,
an urgent siren frightens you.
Nothing to fear,
the imperious moon
moves out from the eaves over us.

Calm, still, you sing again
of eternal love.

LOUISE C. CALLAGHAN

Laburnum

You walk into an ordinary room
on an ordinary evening, say
mid-May, when the laburnum

hangs over the railings of the Square
and the city is lulled by eight o'clock,
the traffic sparse, the air fresher.

You expect to find someone
waiting, though now you live
alone. You've answered none

of your calls. The letters pile
up in the corner. The idea
persists that someone waits while

you turn the brass handle and knock
on the light. Gradually
the dark seeps into the room, you lock

out the night, scan a few books.
It's days since you ate.
The plants are dying — even the cactus,

shrivelled like an old scrotum,
has given up the ghost. There's
a heel of wine in a magnum

you bought, when? The day
before? The day before that?
It's the only way

out. The cold sweats
begin. You knock back a few.
You've no clean clothes left.

He is gone. Say it.
Say it to yourself, to the room.
Say it loud enough to believe it.

You will live breath
by breath. The beat of your own heart
will scourge you. You'll wait

in vain, for he's gone from you.
And every night is a long
slide to the dawn you

wake to, terrified in your ordinary room
on an ordinary morning, say
mid-May, say the time of laburnum.

Paula Meehan

Demeter

Where I lived — winter and hard earth.
I sat in my cold stone room
choosing tough words, granite, flint,

to break the ice. My broken heart —
I tried that but it skimmed,
flat, over the frozen lake.

She came from a long, long way,
but I saw her at last, walking,
my daughter, my girl, across the fields,

in bare feet, bringing all spring's flowers
to her mother's house. I swear
the air softened and warmed as she moved,

the blue sky smiling, none too soon,
with the small shy mouth of a new moon.

CAROL ANN DUFFY

Why Brownlee Left

Why Brownlee left, and where he went,
Is a mystery even now.
For if a man should have been content
It was him; two acres of barley,
One of potatoes, four bullocks,
A milker, a slated farmhouse.
He was last seen going out to plough
On a March morning, bright and early.

By noon Brownlee was famous;
They had found all abandoned, with
The last rig unbroken, his pair of black
Horses, like man and wife,
Shifting their weight from foot to
Foot, and gazing into the future.

PAUL MULDOON

The Portrait

My mother never forgave my father
for killing himself,
especially at such an awkward time
and in a public park,
that spring
when I was waiting to be born.
She locked his name
in her deepest cabinet
and would not let him out,
though I could hear him thumping.
When I came down from the attic
with the pastel portrait in my hand
of a long-lipped stranger
with a brave moustache
and deep brown level eyes,
she ripped it into shreds
without a single word
and slapped me hard.
In my sixty-fourth year
I can feel my cheek
still burning.

STANLEY KUNITZ

Five Flights Up

Still dark.
The unknown bird sits on his usual branch.
The little dog next door barks in his sleep
inquiringly, just once.
Perhaps in his sleep, too, the bird inquires
once or twice, quavering.
Questions — if that is what they are —
answered directly, simply,
by day itself.

Enormous morning, ponderous, meticulous;
grey light streaking each bare branch,
each single twig, along one side,
making another tree, of glassy veins . . .
The bird still sits there. Now he seems to yawn.

The little black dog runs in his yard.
His owner's voice arises, stern,
'You ought to be ashamed!'
What has he done?
He bounces cheerfully up and down;
he rushes in circles in the fallen leaves.

Obviously, he has no sense of shame.
He and the bird know everything is answered,
all taken care of,
no need to ask again.
— Yesterday brought to today so lightly!
(A yesterday I find almost impossible to lift.)

ELIZABETH BISHOP

Deaths and Engines

We came down above the houses
In a stiff curve, and
At the edge of Paris airport
Saw an empty tunnel
— The back half of a plane, black
On the snow, nobody near it,
Tubular, burnt-out and frozen.

When we faced again
The snow-white runways in the dark
No sound came over
The loudspeakers, except the sighs
Of the lonely pilot.

The cold of metal wings is contagious:
Soon you will need wings of your own,
Cornered in the angle where
Time and life like a knife and fork
Cross, and the lifeline in your palm
Breaks, and the curve of an aeroplane's track
Meets the straight skyline.

The images of relief:
Hospital pyjamas, screens round a bed
A man with a bloody face
Sitting up in bed, conversing cheerfully
Through cut lips:
These will fail you some time.

You will find yourself alone
Accelerating down a blind
Alley, too late to stop
And know how light your death is;
You will be scattered like wreckage,
The pieces every one a different shape
Will spin and lodge in the hearts
Of all who love you.

EILÉAN NÍ CHUILLEANÁIN

Tell Me a Story

[A]

Long ago, in Kentucky, I, a boy, stood
By a dirt road, in first dark, and heard
The great geese hoot northward.

    I could not see them, there being no moon
    And the stars sparse. I heard them.

    I did not know what was happening in my heart.

    It was the season before the elderberry blooms.
    Therefore they were going north.

    The sound was passing northward.

[B]

Tell me a story.

In this century, and moment, of mania,
Tell me a story.

Make it a story of great distances, and starlight.

The name of the story will be Time,
But you must not pronounce its name.

Tell me a story of deep delight.

Robert Penn Warren

Nocturne

Time for sleep. Time for a nightcap of grave music,
a dark nocturne, a late quartet, a parting song,
bequeathed by the great dead in perpetuity.

I catch a glance sometimes of my own dead at the
    window,
those whose traits I share: thin as moths, as matchsticks,
they stare into the haven of the warm room, eyes ablaze.

It is Sunday a lifetime ago. A woman in a now-demolished
    house
sings *Michael, Row the Boat Ashore* as she sets down the
    bucket
with its smooth folds of drinking water . . .

The steadfast harvest moon out there, entangled in the
    willow's
stringy hair, directs me home like T'ao Ch'ien: *A caged
bird pines for its first forest, a salmon thirsts for its stream.*

DENNIS O'DRISCOLL

155

from Clearances

In the last minutes he said more to her
Almost than in all their life together.
'You'll be in New Row on Monday night
And I'll come up for you and you'll be glad
When I walk in the door . . . Isn't that right?'
His head was bent down to her propped-up head.
She could not hear but we were overjoyed.
He called her good and girl. Then she was dead.
The searching for a pulsebeat was abandoned.
And we all knew one thing by being there.
The space we stood around had been emptied
Into us to keep, it penetrated
Clearances that suddenly stood open.
High cries were felled and a pure change happened.

SEAMUS HEANEY

Evening Train

An old man sleeping in the evening train,
face upturned, mouth discreetly closed,
hands clasped, with fingers interlaced.
Those large hands
lie on the fur lining of his wife's coat
he's holding for her, and the fur
looks like a limp dog, docile and affectionate.
The man himself is a peasant
in city clothes, moderately prosperous —
rich by the standards of his youth;
one can read that in his hands,
his sleeping features.
How tired he is, how tired.
I called him old, but then I remember
my own age, and acknowledge he's likely
no older than I. But in the dimension
that moves with us but itself keeps still
like the bubble in a carpenter's level,
I'm fourteen, watching the faces I saw each day
on the train going in to London,
and never spoke to; or guessing
from a row of shoes what sort of faces
I'd see if I raised my eyes.
Everyone has an unchanging age (or sometimes two)
carried within them, beyond expression.
This man perhaps
is ten, putting in a few hours most days

in a crowded schoolroom, and a lot more
at work in the fields; a boy who's always
making plans to go fishing his first free day.
The train moves through the dark quite swiftly
(the Italian dark, as it happens)
with its load of people, each
with a conscious destination, each
with a known age and that other,
the hidden one — except for those
still young, or not young but slower to focus,
who haven't reached yet that state of being
which will become
not a point of arrest but a core
around which the mind develops, reflections circle,
events accrue — a centre.
                                   A girl with braids
sits in this corner seat, invisible,
pleased with her solitude. And across from her
an invisible boy, dreaming. She knows
she cannot imagine his dreams. Quite swiftly
we move through our lives; swiftly, steadily the train
rocks and bounces onward through sleeping fields,
our unknown stillness
holding level as water sealed in glass.

DENISE LEVERTOV

158

On Finding an Old Photograph

Yalding, 1912. My father
in an apple orchard, sunlight
patching his stylish bags;

three women dressed in soft
white blouses, skirts that brush the grass;
a child with curly hair.

If they were strangers
it would calm me — half-drugged
by the atmosphere — but it does more —

eases a burden
made of all his sadness
and the things I didn't give him.

There he is, happy, and I am unborn.

WENDY COPE

BC : AD

This was the moment when Before
Turned into After, and the future's
Uninvented timekeepers presented arms.

This was the moment when nothing
Happened. Only dull peace
Sprawled boringly over the earth.

This was the moment when even energetic Romans
Could find nothing better to do
Than counting heads in remote provinces.

And this was the moment
When a few farm workers and three
Members of an obscure Persian sect

Walked haphazard by starlight straight
Into the kingdom of heaven.

U. A. FANTHORPE

The House Was Quiet and the World Was Calm

The house was quiet and the world was calm.
The reader became the book; and summer night

Was like the conscious being of the book.
The house was quiet and the world was calm.

The words were spoken as if there was no book,
Except that the reader leaned above the page,

Wanted to lean, wanted much most to be
The scholar to whom his book is true, to whom

The summer night is like a perfection of thought.
The house was quiet because it had to be.

The quiet was part of the meaning, part of the mind:
The access of perfection to the page.

And the world was calm. The truth in a calm world,
In which there is no other meaning, itself

Is calm, itself is summer and night, itself
Is the reader leaning late and reading there.

WALLACE STEVENS

Paradoxes and Oxymorons

This poem is concerned with language on a very plain
    level.
Look at it talking to you. You look out a window
Or pretend to fidget. You have it but you don't have it.
You miss it, it misses you. You miss each other.

The poem is sad because it wants to be yours, and
    cannot.
What's a plain level? It is that and other things,
Bringing a system of them into play. Play?
Well, actually, yes, but I consider play to be

A deeper outside thing, a dreamed role-pattern,
As in the division of grace these long August days
Without proof. Open-ended. And before you know
It gets lost in the steam and chatter of typewriters.

It has been played once more. I think you exist only
To tease me into doing it, on your level, and then you
    aren't there
Or have adopted a different attitude. And the poem
Has set me softly down beside you. The poem is you.

JOHN ASHBERY

Love After Love

The time will come
when, with elation,
you will greet yourself arriving
at your own door, in your own mirror,
and each will smile at the other's welcome,

and say, sit here. Eat.
You will love again the stranger who was your self.
Give wine. Give bread. Give back your heart
to itself, to the stranger who has loved you

all your life, whom you ignored
for another, who knows you by heart.
Take down the love letters from the bookshelf,

the photographs, the desperate notes,
peel your own image from the mirror.
Sit. Feast on your life.

DEREK WALCOTT

The Dead

The dead are always looking down on us, they say,
while we are putting on our shoes or making a sandwich,
they are looking down through the glass-bottom boats
    of heaven
as they row themselves slowly through eternity.

They watch the tops of our heads moving below on
    earth,
and when we lie down in a field or on a couch,
drugged perhaps by the hum of a warm afternoon,
they think we are looking back at them,

which makes them lift their oars and fall silent
and wait, like parents, for us to close our eyes.

BILLY COLLINS

BIOGRAPHICAL NOTES

Fleur Adcock was born in Auckland, New Zealand in 1934 and has lived in London since 1964. Married at eighteen, she had two sons and got divorced at twenty-four. Laconic is how she described her own poetry. She has published several collections – there is a *Selected Poems 1960 – 2000* – and she has also edited *The Faber Book of Twentieth-Century Women's Poetry* and co-edited *The Oxford Book of Creatures*.

Simon Armitage was born in Huddersfield, West Yorkshire in 1963. He published his first collection, *Zoom!*, in 1989 from which 'November' is taken. Other books include *Kid, Book of Matches, The Dead Sea Poems* and *Cloudcuckooland*. He also edited – with Richard Crawford – *The Penguin Book of Poetry from Britain and Ireland since 1945*. He worked as a probation officer in Marsden and now teaches at the University of Leeds and the University of Iowa.

John Ashbery was born in 1927 in Rochester, New York. Educated at Harvard and Columbia, he published his first book in 1956. He won the National Book Award, Pulitzer Prize and the National Book Critics Circle Prize for *Self-Portrait in a Convex Mirror* in 1976.

W. H. Auden was born in York in 1907. He went to Oxford to study biology, but changed to English. After Oxford, he lived in Germany, but returned to England to teach before becoming a full-time writer. Though homosexual, Auden married Erica Mann – Thomas Mann's daughter – in 1935 because it allowed her an English passport and escape from Nazi persecution. Auden travelled in Spain, and China and settled in New York. He returned to England and was Professor of Poetry at Oxford from 1956 to 1961. He died in 1973.

Elizabeth Bishop, an only child, was born in Worcester, Massachusetts in 1911. Educated at Vassar, she lived in Brazil for many years and travelled all her life. A Pulitzer Prize winner in 1956, she returned permanently to the US in 1972 where she taught at Harvard and MIT.

Eavan Boland was born in Dublin in 1944 but her father's career as a diplomat meant that she spent her early years in London and New York. She boarded at Holy Child Convent, Killiney and attended Trinity College. Eavan Boland published her first book of poems at twenty-two and a *Collected Poems* appeared in 1995. That same year she also published *Object Lessons: The Life of the Woman* and *The Poet in Our Time*. She now teaches at Stanford University, Palo Alto, California.

Pat Boran was born in Portlaoise in 1963 and his book *The Unwound Clock* won the Patrick Kavanagh Award in 1993. He has given many creative writing courses and in 1999 published *The Portable Creative Writing Workshop*. Broadcaster, fiction writer, non-fiction writer, he has published four volumes of poetry including *The Shape of Water* (1996) from which 'Autumn Song' is taken.

Lucy Brennan was born in Dublin in 1931. She grew up in Cork and emigrated to Canada in 1957. She has a Masters Degree in Creative Writing and now lives in Whitby, Ontario. Her first collection, *Migrants All*, was published in Toronto in 1999.

Louise C. Callaghan was born in Dublin in 1948. She studied English and Spanish at UCD and worked in publishing for several years. Her first collection, *The Puzzle-Heart*, appeared in 1999. 'Love Song', included here, was written in Oakland, California.

Moya Cannon was born in Donegal in 1956. She studied History and Politics at UCD and Cambridge and now lives in Galway where she teaches in a school for adolescent travellers. She has published two collections: *Oar* and *The Parchment Boat*.

Charles Causley was born in 1917 in Launceston, Cornwall and he lived there for most of his life. After serving in the Royal Navy during the Second World War, he trained as a teacher. He described his time in the classroom as 'thirty years in chalk Siberias'. *Collected Poems* was published in 1992 and his poem 'Eden Rock' was the final poem in that book.

Amy Clampitt was born in 1920 on a farm in New Providence, Iowa and her poetry career began in 1983 when she published her first collection, *The Kingfisher*, which contains 'The

Reservoirs of Mount Helicon'. Amy Clampitt once described herself as 'a poet of displacement' but she also celebrated the wonders of the natural world. She published five collections in all, and a book of essays. She died in 1994.

Kate Clanchy was born in Glasgow in 1965 and studied at Exeter College, Oxford. She lives in London and works as a teacher and freelance journalist.

Gillian Clarke was born in Cardiff in 1937 and studied English at Cardiff University. She published her first collection in 1971. She worked in broadcasting and as an art historian and was appointed Chair of the Welsh Academy. Her *Collected Poems* appeared in 1997.

Billy Collins was born in New York City in 1941. He has published six collections of poetry, and is Professor of English at Lehman College, New York. He has conducted summer poetry workshops in Galway at the National University for several years. 'Nostalgia' and 'The Dead' are from his 1991 collection *Questions About Angels*. A Selected Poems, *Taking Off Emily Dickinson's Clothes* was published on this side of the Atlantic in 2000.

Wendy Cope was born in 1945 in Kent. She studied history at St Hilda's College, Oxford and taught in a primary school. Her first collection, *Making Cocoa For Kingsley Amis* (1986), sold like hot cakes, as did *Serious Concerns* (1991). She lives in London.

Theo Dorgan was born in Cork in 1953. He was educated at the National University at Cork and is now Director of Poetry Ireland. *The Ordinary House of Love* and *Rosa Mundi* are poetry collections but he has also edited collections of essays and most recently – with Noel Duffy – *Watching The River Flow, A Century of Irish Poetry*. He is also a broadcaster with RTÉ 1 and Lyric FM.

Carol Ann Duffy was born in Glasgow in 1955. She grew up in England and studied philosophy in Liverpool University. She now lives in Manchester and lectures in poetry for the writing school at Manchester Metropolitan University. There are five collections, *Selected Poems* and *Poems Selected and New 1985 - 1999*.

Katherine Duffy was born in Dundalk in 1962. She studied English and Irish at UCD and now lives in Dublin where she works as a librarian. *The Erratic Behaviour of Tides* (1998) is her first collection, from which 'The Great Stretch' is taken.

Noel Duffy was born in Dublin in 1971. He studied physics at Trinity College, Dublin and worked with Poetry Ireland where he edited – with Theo Dorgan – *Watching The River Flow, A Century of Irish Poetry* . He is now writing full time.

Christina Dunhill is a poet and short story writer. She teaches creative writing at the City Literary Institute in London and in private workshops.

Douglas Dunn was born in 1942 in Renfrewshire, Scotland and worked as a librarian, with Philip Larkin, at the University of Hull. His fifth collection, *Elegies*, was written on the death of his wife and won the Whitbread Prize. He was appointed Professor of English at St Andrew's University in 1991.

Paul Durcan was born in Dublin in 1944 and is one of Ireland's best-known and best-loved poets. He has performed his poetry throughout Ireland and in five continents. His most recent book is *Greetings to our Friends in Brazil* (1999). 'Parents' is from his 1978 collection *Sam's Cross*. He has published over fifteen books.

D. J. Enright was born in 1920 in Leamington, Warwickshire and studied English at Cambridge. He taught in Egypt, Japan, West Berlin, Bangkok and Singapore and at Warwick University. Winner of the Queen's Gold Medal for Poetry in 1981, he has published novels and critical works in addition to poetry. His *Collected Poems* was published in 1987.

U. A. Fanthorpe was born in London in 1929. She was educated at Oxford and taught for many years until she became 'a middle-aged drop-out' and worked as a clerk. She published five collections and a *Selected Poems* appeared in 1986. Ursula A. Fanthorpe lives in Gloucestershire.

Louise Glück was born in New York in 1943 and now lives in Vermont. Her collection *The Wild Iris* won the Pulitzer Prize. 'The Magi' is from her 1975 collection, *The House on Marshland*.

Angela Greene was born in England in 1936 but grew up in Dublin. She won the Patrick Kavanagh Award in 1988 and published her only collection in 1993, entitled *Silence and the Blue Night*. She died in 1997.

Eamon Grennan was born in Dublin in 1941. He studied at UCD and Harvard and now teaches at Vassar College, New York State. His poetry collections include *Wildly for Days*, *What Light There Is* (from which 'Four Deer' is taken), *As If It Matters* and *So It Goes*.

Vona Groarke was born in 1964 in Edgeworthstown, County Longford and studied at Trinity College, Dublin and UCC. She has published two collections, *Shale* and *Other People's Houses* and has been writer in residence in both University College, Galway and Maynooth.

Kerry Hardie was born in Singapore in 1951, grew up in County Down and now lives in County Kilkenny. She published her first collection, *A Furious Place*, in 1996 and her second, *Cry for the Hot Belly* in 2000. She was ill for many years with ME and she has written about this – especially in 'She Replies to Carmel's Letter' and 'What's Left' – with clear-sightedness and without self-pity. Her novel, *Hannie Bennet's Winter Marriage*, was also published in 2000.

Tony Harrison was born in 1937 in Leeds. He studied classics at Leeds University. He has lectured in Nigeria and Prague and was resident dramatist at the National Theatre. He has translated several plays and his *Selected Poems* appeared in 1984.

Anne Le Marquand Hartigan was born in 1937 and studied art at Reading University. She has published four collections of poetry (*Long Tongue; Return Single; Now is a Moveable Feast; Immortal Sins*). She has written plays and paints. She has lived in Ireland since 1962 and now lives in Dublin.

Anne Haverty was born in Tipperary in 1959 and studied at Trinity College. She published a biography of Constance Markievicz in 1988 and her 1997 novel, *One Day as a Tiger*, won the Rooney Prize that year. Her first collection of poems is *The Beauty of the Moon* (1999). A second novel, *The Far Side of a Kiss*, was published in 2000.

Seamus Heaney was born in 1939 in County Derry and has earned world-wide fame as poet, critic, lecturer and teacher. He was awarded the Nobel Prize for Literature in 1995. *Opened Ground, Poems 1966 – 1996* was published in 1998. His translation of *Beowulf* won the Whitbread Book of the Year in 1999.

Rita Ann Higgins was born in Galway in 1955. She did not complete a formal education but read widely while recovering from tuberculosis. In 1986 she published her first book of poems, *Goddess on the Mervue Bus*. Other books include *Witch in the Bushes, Goddess and Witch, Philomena's Revenge, Higher Purchase* and *Selected Poems: Sunny Side Plucked*.

Elizabeth Jennings was born in 1926 in Boston, Lincolnshire and studied at Oxford University. She worked in advertising and as a librarian before becoming a full-time writer. A *Collected Poems* was published in 1987.

Thomas Kinsella was born in Dublin in 1928. He studied at UCD and joined the civil service where he worked for nineteen years. After that he held teaching posts in American universities. His *Collected Poems* was published by Oxford University Press.

August Kleinzahler was born in Jersey City, New Jersey in 1949 and he now lives in San Francisco. He has published five collections to date: *Storm Over Hackensack*, *Earthquake Weather*, *Like Cities, Like Storms*, *Red Sauce, Whiskey and Snow* (from which 'Winter Ball' is taken) and *Green Sees Things in Waves*.

Stanley Kunitz was born in 1905 in Worcester, Massachusetts. After Harvard he worked in New York, joined the army for the Second World War, and after the war he held several academic posts. He won a Pulitzer Prize for poetry in 1958.

Philip Larkin was born in Coventry in 1922, studied English at Oxford and worked as a librarian. He spent over half of his life in Hull. His *Collected Poems* was published in 1988, three years after he died.

Denise Levertov was born in England but emigrated to the

United States in 1948. She was Professor of English at Stanford University and published over fifteen collections. *Evening Train* was published in 1992. Denise Levertov died in 1997.

Michael Longley was born in Belfast in 1939 and studied classics at Trinity College, Dublin. He taught in Dublin, London and Belfast and later joined the Arts Council of Northern Ireland. He published his first collection, *No Continuing City*, in 1969 and his most recent book is *The Weather in Japan* (2000) which contains 'A Prayer'.

Thomas Lux was born in Massachusetts in 1946. He now teaches at Sarah Lawrence College in New York. Collections include *Memory's Hand-grenade*, *Glassblower's Breath*, *Sunday*, *Half Promised Land* and *The Drowned River*.

Joan McBreen was born in Sligo in 1944 and now lives in Tuam, County Galway. She has published two collections of poetry, *The Wind Beyond the Wall* and *A Walled Garden* in Moylough. *The White Page, Twentieth Century Irish Women Poets*, which she edited, was published in 1999.

Catherine Phil MacCarthy was born in Crecora, County Limerick in 1954. She published her first collection, *This Hour of the Tide*, in 1994 and, more recently, *The Blue Globe* in 1998. 'Logan' is taken from this second collection.

Liz McSkeane was born in Glasgow in 1956 but moved to Dublin in 1981. A pamphlet of poems, *In Flight*, was published in 1995. 'Snow at the Opera House' was first published in *The Irish Times* in 2000.

Derek Mahon was born in Belfast in 1941 and studied French at Trinity College, Dublin. He taught and worked as a freelance journalist in Ireland and abroad but now lives in Dublin. His *Collected Poems* was published in 1999.

Aidan Mathews was born in 1956 and now works in the Drama Department, RTÉ Radio. He is a novelist, short-story writer and playwright as well as a poet. His three poetry collections are *Windfalls*, *Minding Ruth* and *According to the Small Hours*.

Paula Meehan was born in Dublin in 1955. She was educated at Trinity College and Eastern Washington College in the United States. Her first collection, *Return and No Blame*, was published in 1984. There are four collections, a volume of selected poems, and she has also written plays.

Czeslaw Milosz was born in 1911 in Szetejnie, Lithuania (then in Tsarist Russia) and was brought up in Wilno. He worked for the Resistance during World War II. He spent nearly thirty-five years in exile, first in Paris, then in California where he was appointed Professor of Slavic Languages and Literature at Berkeley. Czeslaw Milosz was awarded the Nobel Prize for Literature in 1980. His *Collected Poems 1931 – 1987* was published in 1988.

John Montague was born in 1929 in New York but grew up in

County Tyrone. He studied at UCD and at the University of Iowa, taught in American universities, lived in Paris for many years and returned to Ireland and a teaching post in UCC in 1974. His *Collected Poems* was published in 1995 and he was appointed to the Ireland Chair of Poetry in 1998. He lives in west Cork.

Marianne Moore was born in 1887 in Missouri and moved to New York in 1918. In 1929 she moved, with her mother, to a fifth-floor apartment on Cumberland Street in Brooklyn where she lived for the rest of their lives. The *Complete Poems* with its famous epigraph 'Omissions are not accidents' was published in 1967. Marianne Moore died in 1972.

Andrew Motion was born in 1952 in London, and studied English at Oxford where he won the Newdigate Prize. His poem 'The Letter' came first out of thirty-five thousand entries in the Arvon/Observer poetry competition in 1981. He published his first collection, *The Pleasure Steamers* in 1978 and has published several collections since. He has written novels, critical works and several biographies, including biographies of Philip Larkin and John Keats. In May 1999 he succeeded Ted Hughes to become Britain's nineteenth Poet Laureate.

Paul Muldoon was born in Portadown, County Armagh in 1951. He attended Queen's University, worked for the BBC in Belfast and moved to the US in the mid 1980s where he is now a professor at Princeton University. He published his first collection, *New Weather*, at twenty-one and his most recent is *Hay* (1998). A *New Selected Poems* was published in 1996.

Eilean Ní Chuilleanáin was born in Cork in 1942. She studied at UCC and at Oxford and now lectures in medieval and renaissance literature at Trinity College. Winner of the Patrick Kavanagh Award in 1973, she has published six collections of poetry: *Acts and Monuments*, *Site of Ambush*, *The Second Voyage*, *The Rose-Geranium*, *The Magdalen Sermon* and *The Brazen Serpent*.

Conor O'Callaghan was born in Newry, County Down in 1968 and his first collection, *The History of Rain*, won the Patrick Kavanagh Award in 1993. A second collection, *Seatown*, was published in 1999. He was writer-in-residence in UCD in 2000 and lives in Dundalk – Seatown is the name given to the oldest part of Dundalk town.

Julie O'Callaghan was born in Chicago in 1954 and now lives in Naas. She has published three collections, *Edible Anecdotes*, *What's What* and *No Can Do* from which 'Alla Luna', written in memory of her father Jack O'Callaghan, is taken. She has also written two books of poetry for younger readers, *Taking My Pen for a Walk* and *Two Barks*.

Bernard O'Donoghue was born in Cullen, County Cork, in 1945. He lives in Oxford where he teaches medieval literature at Wadham College. There are four collections: *Poaching Rights*, *The Weakness*, *Gunpowder* (for which he won the Whitbread Prize) and *Here Nor There*. 'Westering Home' is taken from his most recent book. Bernard O'Donoghue returns to Cullen each year.

Dennis O'Driscoll was born in Thurles in 1954. He works as a civil servant in Dublin and his commitment to poetry is total. He has published five collections, *Kist*, *Hidden Extras*, *Long Short Story*, *Quality Time* and *Weather Permitting*. Both 'In Memory of Alois Alzheimer' and 'Nocturne' are from this last collection.

Sharon Olds was born in San Francisco in 1942 and studied at Stanford and Columbia. She now lives in New York where she teaches at New York University. Her collections include *Satan Says*, *The Dead and the Living*, *The Gold Cell*, *The Father*, *The Wellspring*. 'Looking at Them Asleep' is from *The Gold Cell*.

Ruth Padel was born in 1947 and taught classics at London University. There are four collections: *Summer Snow*, *Angel*, *Fusewire* and *Rembrandt Would Have Loved You*. 'Bed-Time' is from this last collection.

Grace Paley, 'a combative pacifist and cooperative anarchist' was born in New York in 1922. Her books include *Little Disturbances of Man*, *Enormous Changes at the Last Minute*, *Later the Same Day*, *362 Reasons Not to Have Another War*.

Kathleen Raine was born in 1908 in London and grew up in Northumberland.She has published ten volumes of poetry and her *Collected Poems* was published in 1981.

Adrienne Rich's most recent books of poetry are *Dark Fields of the Republic (Poems 1991–1995)* and *Midnight Salvage: (Poems*

1995–1998.) A new selection of her essays, *Arts of the Possible: Essays and Conversations*, will be published in 2001. She has recently been the recipient of the Dorothea Tanning Prize and of the Lannan Foundation Lifetime Achievement Award. She lives in California.

Robin Robertson was born in 1955 and grew up on the north-east coast of Scotland. He works as an editor and lives in London. 'New Gravity' is the first poem in his first collection, *A Painted Field* (1997).

Carol Satyamurti was born in 1939. A *Selected Poems* was published in 1998.

Jo Shapcott was born in London and studied at Trinity College, Dublin, Oxford and Harvard. She has published three collections: *Phrase Book*, *Electroplating the Baby* and *My Life Asleep*. She edited – with Matthew Sweeney – *Emergency Kit: Poems for Strange Times*.

Harvey Shapiro was born in 1924 in Chicago, studied at Yale and Columbia and worked as an editor. His *Selected Poems* was published in 1997.

Stevie Smith was born in 1902 and died in 1971. Named Florence Margaret, she acquired the nickname 'Stevie' in her late teens. She wrote one of the most telling poems of the twentieth century in 'Not Waving But Drowning'. *Stevie Smith, A Selection* was published in 1983.

William Stafford was born in 1914 and grew up in rural Kansas. He was interned in World War II as a conscientious objector. He won the National Book Award for *Traveling through the Dark* and taught for thirty years in Oregon. He died in 1993.

Wallace Stevens was born in 1879 in Reading, Pennsylvania, attended Harvard and worked for an insurance company all his life. He frequently composed poems on his way to work. *Collected Poems* was published in 1954. He died the following year.

John Wakeman won second place in the Cork Literary Review Poetry Competition with his poem 'Beach Cafe: Portugal.' He edited *The Rialto Magazine* and now edits *The Shop*.

Derek Walcott was born in 1930 in St Lucia, West Indies and returned there to teach after university. His *Collected Poems* was published in 1986. He was awarded the Nobel Prize for Literature in 1992.

Robert Penn Warren was born in Guthrie, Kentucky. He wrote both novels and poetry and won Pulitzer Prizes for both. He died in 1989.

Judith Wright was born in 1915 in New South Wales, Australia. She was the first Australian poet to be awarded the Queen's Gold Medal for Poetry. *The Moving Image*, her first collection, was published in 1946 and her most recent, *Going* *on Talking: Tales of a Great Aunt*, poetry for children, was published in 1998.

Enda Wyley was born in Dublin in 1966 where she now teaches. She has an MA in creative writing and has published two collections, *Eating Baby Jesus* and *Socrates in the Garden*.

Index of Titles

Index of First Lines

Copyright Acknowledgements

The editor and publisher gratefully acknowledge permission to use copyright material in this book as follows:

Bloodaxe Books Ltd for 'For Andrew', 'Saturday', 'On a Son Returned to New Zealand' by Fleur Adcock from *Poems 1960–2000* (Bloodaxe Books, 2000); Bloodaxe Books Ltd for 'November' by Simon Armitage from *Zoom!* (Bloodaxe Books, 1989); Carcanet Press Limited for 'Paradoxes and Oxymorons' from *Selected Poems* by John Ashbery; Faber and Faber Ltd for 'A Summer Night' from *Collected Shorter Poems* by W. H. Auden; Farrar Straus and Giroux, LLC, for permission to reproduce 'It Is Marvellous to Wake Up Together' by Elizabeth Bishop. First appeared in April Vol 17 #1 of *American Poetry Review*. Copyright ©1988 by Alice Helen Methfessel. 'Five Flights Up' from *The Complete Poems 1927–1979* by Elizabeth Bishop. Copyright ©1979, 1983 by Alice Helen Methfessel; Carcanet Press Limited for 'Nocturne' from *Selected Poems* by Eavan Boland; Pat Boran and the Dedalus Press for 'Autumn Song' from *The Shape of Water*; Lucy Brennan for 'When All is Said and Done'; Louise C. Callaghan for 'Love Song'; Moya Cannon and The Gallery Press for 'Crow's Nest' from *Oar*; David Higham Associates for 'Eden Rock' from *Collected Poems 1951–2000* (Macmillan, 2000) by Charles Causley; Faber and Faber Ltd for 'The Reservoirs of Mount Helicon' from *Collected Poems* by Amy Clampitt; Kate Clanchy and Chatto & Windus for 'Timetable' from *Slattern*; Carcanet Press Limited for 'The Sundial' from *Collected Poems* by Gillian Clarke; Billy Collins for 'Nostalgia' and 'The Dead'; Faber and Faber for 'On Finding an Old Photograph' by Wendy Cope from *Making Cocoa for Kingsley Amis* (1986); Theo Dorgan for 'Sunday Afternoon'; Carol Ann Duffy for 'Dark School'; Macmillan Publishers Ltd for 'Demeter' by Carol Ann Duffy from *The World's Wife*; 'The Way My Mother Speaks' from *The Other Country* by Carol Ann Duffy published by Anvil Press Poetry in 1990: new edition published in 1998; Katherine Duffy and the Dedalus Press for 'The Great Stretch' from *The Erratic Behaviour of Tides*; Noel Duffy for 'Bella'; Christina Dunhill for 'Old People'; Faber and Faber Ltd for 'Reading Pascal in the Lowlands' from *Selected Poems* by Douglas Dunn; 'Parents' from *A Snail in My Prime* by Paul Durcan. First published in Great Britain in 1993 by Harvill. Copyright ©Paul Durcan, 1993. Reproduced by permission of